TRAMS THROUGH
The Belgian Coastal Tram

Geoffrey Skelsey
and
Yves-Laurent Hansart

ISBN: 978-0-948106-38-5

Written and illustrated by Geoffrey Skelsey and Yves-Laurent Hansart, with additional photographs as credited.

Production Editor: S E Graves

Published by the Light Rail Transit Association

Printed by: Wyndeham Gait, Victoria Street, Grimsby DN31 1PY

Copyright: © Geoffrey Brian Skelsey and Yves-Laurent Hansart, 2010.

"Mijn platte land, mijn Vlaanderland"
["My flat land! My Flanders-land!"]
Jacques Brel, 'Marieke'.

Trams in the dunes: this 1966 view typifies the Coast Line in that era. The 'Route Royale' is still single carriageway and private cars are scattered on its verge whilst holiday-makers sun themselves on the sand hills. The trains consist of type 'SO' motors, each hauling pairs of standard trailers, with characteristic clouds of dry sand thrown up in their wake. A perfect August day.

CONTENTS

Foreword 4

1. Introduction: the geography of the Coast and development of tourism 6

2. From the first steam tram to *SELVOP*, 1885 - 1926 8
    2.1 Preface
    2.2 The Vicinal
    2.3 The first coastal lines
    2.4 Electric traction arrives: 'Compagnie North'
    2.5 Holiday trams eastwards: 'OB'
    2.6 Some exceptions: horses by the sea
    2.7 War and aftermath

Interlude: The Great War and the Vicinal 16

3. Urban trams in Oostende and Knokke 18
    3.1 Preface
    3.2 Oostende town tramways 1885 – 1958
    3.3 Knokke
    3.4 Rolling stock
    3.5 The end of town trams and re-routing in Oostende

4. *SELVOP* and the completion of the coastal chain, 1927 – 1955 23
    4.1 Preface
    4.2 Electrification completed
    4.3 Operation
    4.4 War again
    4.5 Post-war optimism, and reality
    4.6 *SELVOP* expires

**5. 'Threats and opportunities':
revival, the end of the Vicinal, and the coming of De Lijn, 1956 – 2008** 36
    5.1 Preface
    5.2 The SO-series and threats to the future

    5.3 Upgrading and renewal
    5.4 Preparing for the BN's
    5.5 The end of the Vicinal
    5.6 Further improvement and extensions

6. Rolling stock **69**
    6.1 Steam equipment
    6.2 Electric traction: general considerations
    6.3 Pre-1914 electric cars
    6.4 Additional cars, 1914 - 29
    6.5 The bogie revolution
    6.6 The 'Coast Standard' cars
    6.7 Other standards
    6.8 Type SO
    6.9 Trailers
    6.10 Type 'NO' trailers
    6.11 The BN series

7. Looking forward: present and future **92**
    7.1 De Lijn's achievement
    7.2 Future prospects

8. Acknowledgements and Bibliography **100**

Maps
1.   *LNER map of North Sea routes showing Belgian Coast and tramways* 8
2.   *Chronological map 1885 – 2010* 11
3.   *Early routes through Oostende 1885 – 1897* 14
4.   *German military map, Nieuwpoort area 1914* 17
5.   *Oostende town tramways* 18
6.   *Central Oostende showing track alterations June 1954* 22
7.   *Progress of electrification 1897 – 1934* 24
8.   *Development of routes around Nieuwpoort 1885 - 1930* 26

A view over the motorman's shoulder which every traveller on the Coast Line will recall: an S0 motor heads through the sand between De Haan and Wenduine in August 1967. Much of the route was built as single line but was doubled between the wars.
[Tony Percival]

Foreword

Over the last 125 years many thousands of British holidaymakers have caught their first glimpse of a European tram on the quayside at Oostende. More recently, for a generation or so, the Belgian coastal tramway was the nearest modern tramway to south-east England, and its fortunes were keenly followed by a discerning clientele. The Vicinal was always a highly eclectic undertaking, but the coastal lines had a strong character of their own, attuned both to the massive summer holiday traffic of carefree bathers and campers, and to the more modest needs of chilly and misty winter days. Some of the old atmosphere remains in 2010, although both the trams and the built environment in which they run have changed utterly, especially over the last half century. There is certainly little now that would be familiar to the Victorian and Edwardian tourists who rocked their way through the sand dunes on trains of open-ended four-wheeled trams.

One of authors enjoyed just the experience set out above when he arrived at Oostende in a Belgian Marine mail boat in March 1959 and first set eyes on the cream-coloured tram with its gaggle of trailers. His ride to Zeebrugge Mole was his first experience of an undertaking which entranced him then and has done so ever since, with life-changing consequences. He found that this tram was a creature of differing dispositions, utterly unlike the homelier, street-bound sisters he knew in Leeds and Toronto. Now racing excitingly at top speed through the sand hills and alongside broad and empty beaches, then inching through the impatient traffic of Nieuwpoort or Blankenberge, the Coast tram changed its character several times in its nearly three-hour journey. In part it was an aural experience: the conductors' piercing whistles, the distinctive two-tone horn as the tram challenged impeding motorists, the screech of many wheels on curves. A long Vicinal train grinding through town streets was not easily overlooked or soon forgotten.

When the first tram left the Oostende quayside in 1885 the mail boat service had been running for barely forty years and Queen Victoria had another fifteen years to reign (and King Léopold II twenty-four). The cataclysmic events of the next century, which as we shall see profoundly affected Belgium and this tramway in particular, were unimaginable in what seemed to be an era of limitless progress of which the new tramway was but one instance. The 'Flemish Coast Tram' has adapted constantly, and has triumphantly survived the trauma of two World Wars and more: in different form it continues today to serve the needs of the 'sunshine coast' and its visitors. This book describes its origins and development, its rolling stock and electrification, and looks forward to the prosperous future which is surely now assured.

Authors' notes

Language. Although many of the early coastal tramways had French titles, and the language was often used along the Coast as late as the 1950s, linguistic autonomy has long eclipsed it here and it is right that we follow customary usage in adopting the Flemish names of places, even if some are less familiar to many monoglot Britons. 'Flanders', 'Brussels', and 'Belgium' have survived, as apologetic Anglicisms. Names elsewhere are given their local spellings.

There are, however, problems with the familiar name for the national light railway undertaking as a whole. So commonplace is the French term 'Vicinal' in Great Britain, that we have chosen it in preference to the Flemish equivalent 'boerentram'. The abbreviated formulation 'NMVB/SNCV' is also, we hope, permissible, but 'MEBOBB/SELVOP' is maybe a step too far and we note that Flemish writers have used 'SELVOP' alone, by which the tongue-twisting name of the former operating company was usually known.

Orientation. The coastal tramway runs roughly west-south-west to east-north-east, heading about 67 degrees from De Panne to Knokke, but to use this terminology repeatedly is tedious so we have generally chosen the conventional terms 'south-west' and 'north-east' of Oostende.

Dates necessarily loom large in this story but are quoted with considerable reservation, as many are cited differently in the sources. They should be treated with reserve.

Some **photographs** are not of the highest quality, but have been included because of their historical importance. Some 'snaps' are also published because they express perfectly the seaside atmosphere of former times. It has not been possible to identify the photographers in all cases but the authors will be glad to correct attributions in future.

Geoffrey Skelsey, Cambridge
Yves-Laurent Hansart, Brussels
April – September 2009

Geoffrey Skelsey's first photograph of a Vicinal train, at Blankenberge in March 1959. Off-season the SO motor is hauling only a luggage van for mail and parcels.

1. Introduction: the geography of the Coast and development of tourism

It helps in understanding the development and survival of the tramway briefly to consider the physical and social environment within which it operates.

The Belgian North Sea Coast between the frontiers of France and the Netherlands is one of the leading holiday areas of Europe, developed largely over the last hundred years. Although some areas are now protected and retain their original dune landscape, many of the onetime fishing villages and small resorts have mushroomed into contiguous settlements of high-rise apartments and hotels. Building is now continuous over several stretches of the Coast, and only around half remains of the original 6,000 hectares of dunes. The beaches are broad and sandy, and increase in extent from north-east to south-west (around 250 metres wide at Heist and 500 metres at De Panne). The dunes are also broader and attain their greatest height in the south-west, reaching 33 metres near Koksijde. These broad sandhills mean that the old road and its villages ('dorps') are further from the sea in the south-west: as the maps show, each old-established settlement there became matched by a new beach resort ('bad', literally 'bathing place' but perhaps 'beach' or 'shore' will mean more to British readers). Such twin settlements were joined first by roads perpendicular to the Coast (Adinkerke – De Panne in 1892, and Koksijde (Dorp) – (Bad) in 1895, for instance), and later by tramways. This twinning became the distinctive pattern of settlement and transport in the south-west of the Coast, and opened up new areas for select development: the first hotel in De Panne opened in 1893. By 1995 building was almost continuous between Nieuwpoort (Bad) and De Panne where a century earlier there had been nothing but sand. Apart from massive building

Even in 1967 sections of the Coast were relatively unspoiled. A train speeds eastwards near Bredene, passing through the dune landscape which would soon be altered by road construction.
[Tony Percival]

development the topography of dunes and of the land immediately inland is largely artificial and has been greatly modified and stabilised by human intervention. The inland areas, partly 'polders' reclaimed from the sea, are highly fertile, an incentive to provide light railways to carry valuable agricultural produce rapidly and smoothly to market. One very obvious but perhaps overlooked feature of the landscape has influenced the tramways' rolling stock and operations: the land beyond the dunes is flat, the 'flat land' ('plat pays' or 'platte land') of Jacques Brel's song. The design (and power) of rolling stock, and the nearly century-long coastal practice of many-trailered operation with relatively small motor-cars, would have been different had the route not been largely level.

Oostende, the largest individual settlement on the Belgian Coast, has a long history and grew rapidly as a cosmopolitan holiday resort after 1865 when the fortifications were removed, opening up extensive areas for building. Here, and at other points along the Coast, access and hence development were made possible by the arrival of railways (Oostende 1838, Veurne 1858, Blankenberge 1863, Nieuwpoort 1867, Heist 1868, Adinkerke 1870). It is no coincidence that, as we shall see, these were precisely the places initially connected by tramways. Railway development was largely radial, with lines joining the Coast to inland towns. The tramways were lateral, joining the coastal towns together. Holiday and excursion traffic was encouraged by the introduction of a compulsory weekly holiday in Belgium in 1905, and of annual holidays with pay in 1936 (earlier than in the United Kingdom): this changed the predominant social status of visitors.

Both railways and tramways have been extensively modernised since the Second World War, and the arrival of the motorway at Oostende from Brussels in 1954 facilitated still wider access but brought growing traffic problems as we shall see. Oostende and Knokke have also been especially popular with British tourists, fostered by the Belgian state mail steamers joining Dover with Oostende from 1846, and later by other operators from London, and from Harwich and Hull to Zeebrugge.

From the quaysides the tramways distributed holiday-makers, and British railway companies offered through bookings to coastal tramway stations as well as facilities for registered luggage. The Belgian Marine administration transferred their British terminal from Dover to Ramsgate in 1993 but the undertaking was sold off in 1997: foot-passengers are sadly no longer carried.

Industrial development on the Coast brought all-year-round traffic, encouraged by the growth of Zeebrugge as a port, fostered by the British L&NER which introduced train ferries from Harwich in 1924.

At one time many hotels, and even tramways, customarily closed each year outside the main holiday season. Amongst recent factors influencing the tramway favourably has been the extension of the season, facilitated by easier transport and hence readier access for short breaks.

The ever-denser urban development along the Coast has also helped because the summer resident population now overstrains the road system and as elsewhere reinforces the attractions of good-quality public transport, especially where it is insulated from traffic congestion as most of the coastal tramway now is.

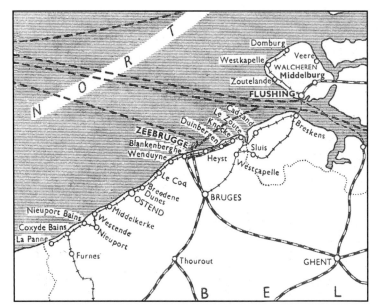

Map 1: General coast map
British railways offered through tickets to coastal tramway points, and this 1937 map shows the LNER's Harwich to Zeebrugge service and connecting tram routes. Remarkably there were bookings to the Dutch towns of Flushing (Vlissingen) and Middelburg using the SBM steam trams and the Breskens ferry. Individual travellers were adventurous then! The map also locates the main points along the coast: note that as was then customary in Great Britain the French forms of place names are given.

2. From the first steam tram to *SELVOP* 1885 - 1926

2.1 Preface
Riding on the Coast Line today the traveller may assume that it was the outcome of an incremental, long-term plan. Well-engineered double track and modern overhead line equipment; the route passing attractively beside the sands and through a succession of busy holiday resorts; much of it running beside or in the centre of a dual-carriageway highway: this seems to tell of a consistent strategy.

In fact nothing could be less true. The present 69 km metre-gauge Coast Line is made up of a dozen different elements, mainly assembled between the world wars from sections built for quite different reasons, and not completed as a through route until 1929. Although the route celebrates its 125th anniversary in 2010 little more than a kilometre of the present line actually dates from 1885, and major parts of the original route, including its approaches to Oostende from each direction, have long disappeared. Through electric trams the length of the Coast did not start until 1931, and the system reached its present extent only in 1998. Some non-electric operation lasted until 1951, and three different forms of traction once ran simultaneously at different points on the route, as described later.

Whilst it is true that 'the tram made the coast' (in the words of the historian Raymond Vancraeynest), that was not the intention behind the first tramway. As already described, the tourist industry was little developed along the Belgian littoral until the 1880s. Apart from the sophisticated international delights of Oostende itself, and to a lesser extent of Blankenberge, there was mainly little more than a scattering of small homes and fishing shacks. Economic activity lay inland, in the reclaimed polders on the landward side of the long range of dunes which stretch almost 150 kilometres through coastal France, Belgium, and the Netherlands. So the purpose behind the first tramways was that of most of early Belgian light railways, fostering economic development by improving links between the countryside and the growing industrial cities.

The Chronological Map (page 11) will identify the main places served and help to follow the sequence of tramway developments described in the next sections. A table summarising the composition of the present coastal line appears on page 28.

2.2 'The Vicinal'

Before we embark on the long path which led to today's coastal tramway we need to look at the statutory structure which made it possible. The *Nationale Maatschappij van Buurtspoorwegen (NMVB) in Flemish, (Société Nationale des Chemins de Fer Vicinaux (SNCV) in French),* ('National Local Railway Undertaking') was established by Royal Decree in 1885, with the duty to 'control the construction and working of a national system of light railways, in association with communes and provinces'. The purpose was to foster economic development of rural areas by providing cheap and reliable local transport beyond existing rail-heads, of special benefit to market-gardening and agriculture. The 'Vicinal' was particularly successful in maintaining economical construction standards, resulting in a far lower cost per kilometre than equivalent British lines (even narrow-gauge). Operating ratios were also favourable before the advent of road transport, and there is convincing evidence that light railways greatly improved the districts they served. 'Belgium eventually possessed the most successful European example of a centrally planned and implemented network of secondary rail transport, supplementing a planned main-line rail system'. By 1913 Belgium possessed 12 km of railway, including the Vicinal, per 10,000 inhabitants, compared with 7.5 km in Great Britain and 9.3 km in Germany.

The Vicinal's responsibilities were to raise the capital, manage construction, and supply equipment to the lines it authorised. It also equalized profit and loss across the whole system, covering deficits on one line by profits on others. Finally, it established universal constructional and operating standards, which enabled rolling stock to be exchanged between concessions, as indeed happened in the case of the coastal lines and which was of special benefit during the two world wars.

Thus the Vicinal secured construction of most of the lines described in this book, and as it happens the very first concession to open an operating tramway was for the line between Oostende and Nieuwpoort. Other local lines were independently financed and built but eventually taken under Vicinal control. Even the modest horse tramways at Knokke and De Panne were absorbed and replaced by metre-gauge electric lines. The Vicinal was not originally intended to operate tramways itself, but to put the lines it had created out to competitive tender. This it did until 1914, but the destruction experienced during the war, and cost increases afterwards, so badly damaged the finances of many concessionaires that the Vicinal was forced to intervene, and increasingly took direct control as concessions expired. The coastal lines remained a concessionary operation until the end of 1955, almost the last to survive.

2.3 The first coastal lines

Our history begins south-west from Oostende, with the construction of a road-based metre-gauge line to the old fishing port of Nieuwpoort at the mouth of the

IJzer (Yser) River. This opened in 1885, and was extended to Koksijde and Veurne the following year. The line linked with the main line railway at each end and at Nieuwpoort. It hardly came within sight of the sea in its entire 32 km length, but instead connected the chain of agricultural and fishing villages which had grown up in the lee of the dunes, then more of an obstacle than an attraction. The Vicinal conceded operation to *La Compagnie Générale des Railways* [sic] *à Voie Etroite* ['General Narrow-gauge Railways Co'], a subsidiary of the better known *Railways Economiques de Liège – Seraing et Extensions* ('RELSE') which survived into modern times. In 1886 a second line out of Oostende also opened, this time north-eastwards through Bredene village to De Haan, Wenduine, and Blankenberge (the last established as a sea-bathing resort from the 1840s, but lacking direct rail connection to Oostende). This second tramway left Oostende well to landward of the dunes, but beyond De Haan the dunes and beaches are shallower and subsequent development was different with the tramway running closer to the sea throughout. This line, connected to the first, was also conceded to *RELSE*.

Just four years later another steam tramway came to the Coast, initially unconnected with the two previous lines. In 1890 a line from the historic city of Brugge reached northwards to the village of Knokke, and then along the Coast to Heist, the terminus of a main line railway since 1868. The Brugge line included a branch eastwards from the village of Westkappelle to the Dutch border at Anna ter Muiden, where a running connection was made with the Dutch *Stoomtram-Maatschappij Breskens – Maldeghem* (SBM), built to metre gauge to facilitate connection with the NMVB/SNCV which it eventually met at three places. The Belgian steam trams operated from Heist or Knokke beyond the border over SBM tracks to the town of Sluis. Meanwhile in the south-west a branch of the Oostende – Veurne steam line was built down the IJzer estuary from Nieuwpoort (Stad) to the new seaside settlement of Nieuwpoort (Bad), opening in 1889, initially partly over mixed-gauge track shared with the West Belgian Railway Company. The Veurne terminus of the Oostende line was joined from 1901 by long new lines southwards to Poperinge and Ieper. Veurne was also linked to De Panne.

Significantly all these steam tramways connected directly with main line railways, and there were branches into the Oostende and Blankenberge railway goods yards. Here the district's agricultural produce could be sent off to the towns, and inbound coal transhipped into narrow-gauge wagons for carriage to the growing number of homes along the Coast. Most intermediate points along the tramway had goods sidings and there were many spurs into industrial premises. Dockside sidings were later installed at Nieuwpoort for rail/ship transfer.

It is interesting to note that across the border French metre-gauge railways were also developing at this period, including a line paralleling the frontier and terminating at Bray Dunes just south-west of De Panne. This 'CF du Nord de la France' opened in 1903, and as we shall see was briefly linked to the Vicinal in 1915.

2.4 Electric traction arrives: The 'Compagnie North'

For almost ten years the infant tram system remained confined to these three lines, i.e.

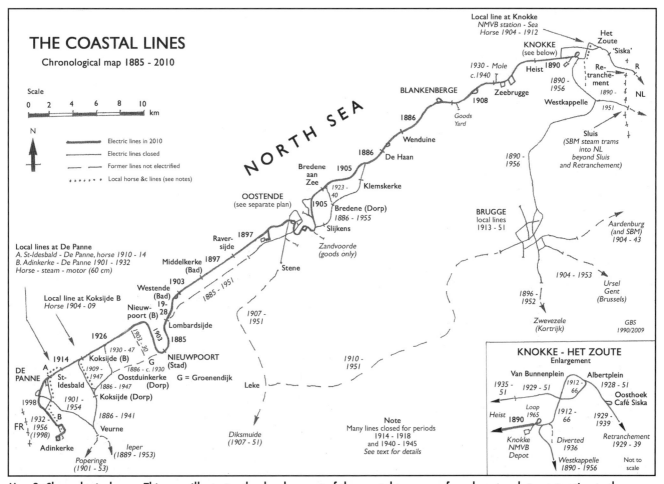

Map 2: Chronological map. This map illustrates the development of the coastal tramways from horse and steam traction to the present light rail line and its latest extension.

south-west and north-east of Oostende, with a third between Heist and Brugge. When building began again it was with a quite different purpose, and began recognisably to lay the foundations of the present Coast Line. Oostende itself, a high-class resort, grew rapidly towards the end of the nineteenth century, in particular expanding south-westwards along the sea wall with its neighbouring stretches of open sandy beach and ample bracing air. It was along this sea wall that the next tramway was built, sponsored by John Thomas North, by origin a Leeds coal-merchant's son, who was a personal friend of King Léopold and of Edward, Prince of Wales with a fortune made from exploiting Latin American nitrate deposits. He also had business interests in Belgium which no doubt inspired his final speculation: his wealth and connections secured him an operating concession independently of the Vicinal.

By 1896, when construction of the line began, an electric tramway had become an attractive and practical proposition, with associations of cleanliness and modernity which appealed especially to the authorities of progressive resorts. It is no coincidence that Oostende, and such places as the Isle of Man, Brighton, and Blackpool amongst

The 'Compagnie North' (TEOL) operated their 1897 line between Oostende and Middelkerke with fourteen modest and angular four-wheeled motor trams, their match-boarded sides giving them the nickname 'teaks'. This early view, in the line's independent days, shows the single track beside the sea, the original trolley poles, and the initial fleet numbers.

many others, embraced electric traction in this era. So the first electric line on the Coast opened along the sea shore between Oostende and Middelkerke (Bad) in the summer of 1897: Middelkerke (Dorp) –'village'- lay inland on the other side of the dunes and was already served by the decade-old steam tramway. North had died suddenly in May 1896 after eating oysters at a London restaurant, but his tramway prospered and was extended south-west in 1903, to the rising resort of Westende (Bad), and there it terminated for over twenty years. The operating company was named *La Compagnie des Tramways Electriques d'Ostende – Littoral* (TEOL), but was commonly called the Compagnie North: indeed a street beside the present tramway in Oostende is still named *'Northlaan'* after this unlikely traction entrepreneur. The TEOL was bought by the Vicinal in 1905 and partly rebuilt and re-aligned before being conceded to the operators of a new eastwards line described below.

Still steam worked, the mixed-gauge branch to Nieuwpoort (Bad) was replaced in 1903 by a parallel metre-gauge line: this was extended a short distance westwards along the Coast and then turned back inland to form a coastal loop before rejoining the main line at Groenendijk. This initially operated in summer only. A further long-distance steam tramway from Diksmuide entered Oostende from the south in 1907, subject always to a separate concession.

2.5 Holiday trams eastwards: The 'OB'

North-east of Oostende resort development had been slower than to the south-west, but here too the Coast was ripe for development and in 1905 a new line was opened from Oostende to De Haan, well to seaward of the original steam line which it joined before De Haan. It is indicative of the nature of the traffic carried, and of the general lack of development along the Coast, that these newer seaside lines both north-east and south-west of Oostende initially operated during the summer season only. The Oostende – De Haan – Blankenberge line

The OB electric line north-east of Oostende opened in 1905 - 08, and one of its early motor trams is seen in Wenduine village. Notice the rotatable bow-collector and the huge oil headlamps. The exceptional width of the tram is also apparent from this viewpoint. These 'OB' cars, altered in detail, remained in service until the 1950s.

The Sea Dyke at Oostende was the route of the first steam route towards Nieuwpoort. This turn-of-the-century view shows it before electrification and the distant tram is one of the accumulator cars introduced in 1897. Some, heavily rebuilt, survived into the 1950s. The Hotel de l'Estacade ('sea-wall' or 'dyke') advertises its services in French, German, and English, but notably not Flemish: in 1910 Baedeker described it dismissively as 'unpretending'. [Courtesy MUPDOFER]

was converted to electric traction in 1909, giving Oostende electric tramways in both directions along the Coast, and consequently making possible an urban tramway system which is described in chapter 3. The original

Visitors to Oostende today will be astonished by this scene although the present Coast Line passes in front of the dock in the background. This is the square outside the original main station, the centre of Vicinal operations until 1954. The elaborate shelter and office in the centre survived until the end of World War II: a similar but smaller one remains in Marie-Joséplein. The typical tram train in the foreground is heading towards Knokke, with a mixture of closed and open trailers.

route via Bredene village was also at least partly worked electrically by the end of 1909. The new Oostende – Blankenberge line was conceded to a new operating company La *SA du Chemin de Fer Electrique d'Ostende – Blankenberghe et extensions* ('OB'), which also operated the Westende line and was another subsidiary of *RELSE*. In effect all these Oostende-based tramways were under the same management, although they ran under different operating contracts, but in 1906 the arrangements were formalised into a single fifty year concession of all the lines to the OB, expiring on 31 December 1955.

In 1908 the Oostende - Blankenberge line was extended further eastwards to Zeebrugge and Heist, thus joining the existing Brugge line and opening up, in theory, a chain of tramways from De Panne through Oostende to Knokke, although it will be seen from the map that much of the route differed from the present one, and a journey the full length would have been a gruelling experience. The line between

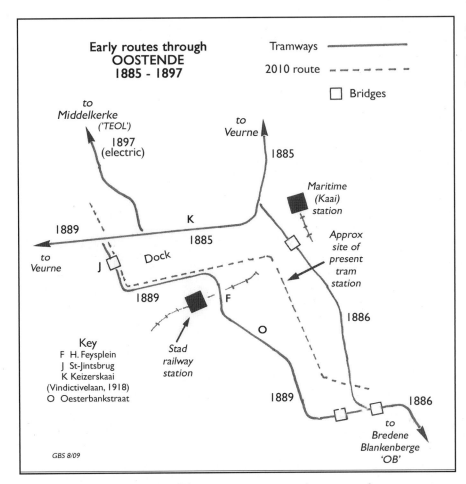

Map 3:
This diagram shows the connections between the first tramways in Oostende and their relation to the present route.

Blankenberge and Knokke was converted to electric traction by 1911-12, thus opening a through electric route to the north-east of Oostende, though the main westerly line remained steam worked. All three tramways were already connected in central Oostende, and the existing steam depot in Nieuwpoortsesteenweg was adapted and extended in 1908 to house the new electric fleet: it was still in use in 2009.

2.6 Some exceptions: horses by the sea

In addition to these 'main-line' tramways, short seasonal lines also appeared along the Coast early in the century, some bridging the gaps between the older villages and the sea. There were three horse tramways in the south-west, between Adinkerke railway station and the seaside at De Panne; along the Coast between De Panne and St-Idesbald; and joining Koksijde (Dorp) to its twin on the Coast. All these lines were associated with property development, to encourage building and holidaying on the Coast. At the other end of the Coast, the village of Knokke underwent rapid development early in the last century, encouraged by the interest of the King whose summer residence was there and who founded one of the leading golf clubs in continental Europe. Here too a horse tramway opened in 1904 joining the station on the Brugge – Heist steam tramway to the beach. The horse line to Koksijde (Bad) was replaced by a new steam-worked Vicinal branch in 1909, and the similar Knokke line

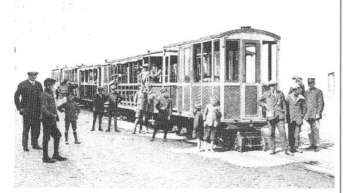

The Adinkerke to De Panne line was an independent 60 cm-gauge tramway, originally worked by horse and later by steam. After the Great War former military petrol tractors were used until the Vicinal replaced the undertaking with a new electrified branch in 1932. This view at De Panne appears to date from the immediate post-war period.

was taken over and electrified in 1912. In 1914 the sea-front horse line at De Panne was replaced by a Vicinal extension, from Koksijde (Bad) through St-Idesbald to De Panne, with the intention of linking with the French metre-gauge Bray Dunes – Hondschoote line and extending beyond Bray to meet the Dunkerque tramways, electrically worked since 1903. By the summer of 1914 only the Adinkerke – De Panne horse line remained outside Vicinal control, but events would soon ensure its survival in original 60 cm-gauge form for another eighteen years, although latterly worked by small petrol locomotives.

2.7 War and its aftermath

No doubt further development would have followed, but as explained in the following 'interlude', the outbreak of general European War on 4 August 1914 brought these, and innumerable other hopes and intentions, to an abrupt end. By cruel mischance one of the most hotly-contested areas on the western battle front lay on and around the coastal tramway, the area between Nieuwpoort and De Panne being the only portion of the Belgian coast to escape occupation. The tramways in that zone were turned over to military use and played a critical role in supplying the Belgian and British armies, connected by other existing steam tramways to the notorious leper battlefields. When peace returned to Belgium at the end of 1918 much of the coastal tram system was largely wrecked. Its restoration is described in chapter 4, together with the creation of a new concessionary operator for the whole system.

The details of the 'Great War' (as it was known) were so influential and long-lasting that they deserve separate treatment. We shall resume our story of the developing tramway later.

This wonderfully-evocative postcard scene at Zeebrugge between the wars shows an eastbound train with four-wheeled trailer No 11577 at the rear. This was one of twenty similar cars built in 1909, remaining in service until the 1950s. Notice the large oil tail lamp: a legal requirement meant that these continued to be carried, even by modern cars, until the 1960s. In the foreground one of the 'receveurs' (conductors), cash bag strapped round his shoulder, waits to signal the train on its way.

Interlude - The Great War and the Vicinal

As much as any other surviving tramway, the Coastal Line was profoundly affected by the two world wars of the twentieth century. When Germany invaded Belgium on 2 August 1914, as part of a strategy to prevent France from supporting its ally Russia, the action triggered a series of treaty obligations which precipitated global conflict. The crucial obligation was that of the United Kingdom which had guaranteed Belgian neutrality at the birth of the new State, specifically by Article 7 of the Treaty of London 1839, the 'scrap of paper' contemptuously dismissed by the German Kaiser. Although much delayed by heroic resistance, the German armies far exceeded the strength of the Belgians and most of the country was occupied by the autumn (Brussels on 20 August, Oostende on 15 October). Much of the occupied Coast was then fortified, especially at Zeebrugge and Oostende, which were bases for submarine and torpedo-boat operations against the British. All tramways south-west of Oostende were closed to the public by 13 October 1914.

However the Belgian army fell back on the IJzer River and joined French and British forces in defending a small national enclave west of a line joining Nieuwpoort with Armentières, partly secured by inundating land along the IJzer to prevent German advance. Despite appalling fighting this area was never captured, and Nieuwpoort remained the North Sea end of the 600 mile [965 km] long Western Front for the remainder of the war. Providently much Vicinal rolling stock had been withdrawn westwards in the early autumn and a sizeable fleet was able to operate within the Belgian-British zone, under military control and operated by a newly-constituted *'Section Vicinale des Chemins de Fer en Campagne'* with headquarters at Veurne. Additional new locomotives and wagons were subsequently supplied from Great Britain and the USA.

The Vicinal main line west of Oostende was broken in 1914 between Westende and Oostduinkerke, and in the occupied zone was supplemented by a new metre-gauge military railway linking Westende with Leffinghe. In the Allied zone the Veurne – Ieper and Veurne – Poperinge lines remained in use together with a metre-gauge network joining Oostduinkerke, Veurne, De Panne, and Koksijde (Bad). A complex system of 60 cm gauge lines was added between Koksijde and Nieuwpoort, feeding the front line.

In the north-east the line was badly damaged by German operations and by British bombardment and raids on Oostende and Zeebrugge, especially in 1918. Damage might have been far worse: at one stage the Allies planned a major sea-borne landing between Raversijde and Westende to relieve Ieper, which would have been immensely destructive, as in northern France in 1944.

An interesting aspect of the Allied military railway system was the construction of cross-border metre-gauge lines in 1915, one linking Houtem (between Veurne and Poperinge) with Pont au Cerf on the French *CF du Nord de la France* line. Lacking the central organization and universal technical standards of the Vicinal the French metre-gauge lines faced great difficulties in inter-working rolling stock, and the international links did not survive the war. The Vicinal formed the vital core of Allied military railways the length of the Ypres front.

At the end of the war the task of restoration facing the Belgian Government was almost beyond belief. The longer-distance lines into the interior, from Oostende to Diksmuide and Veurne to Ieper and Poperinge, were open to the public again by the middle of 1919, but elsewhere in Flanders reconstruction was not complete until 1923. Although it is hard to find a silver lining in such dire events, the Vicinal did benefit by receiving war-surplus steam locomotives, as well as many goods wagons. A lesser acquisition was a petrol tractor of the 'Simplex' type which took over operations on the 60cm gauge Adinkerke – De Panne line (similar machines worked on some British narrow gauge lines). The table summarises reopening of the coastal lines.

Date	Section
by March 1919	Brugge – Heist
June 1919	Knokke – Het Zoute
by June 1919	Oostende – De Haan – Heist
by August 1919	Oostende – Mariakerke (Dorp) – Veurne
October 1920	Koksijde (Dorp) – St-Idesbald – De Panne
January 1921	Westkapelle – Sluis
by September 1921	Oostende – Westende (Bad)
1919 – 1921	Oostende local routes

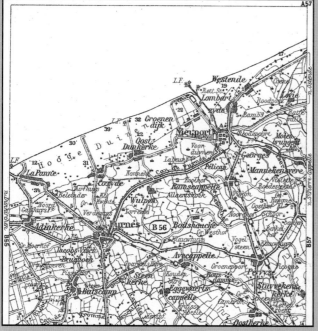

Map 4. This section of a German military map published c. 1915 includes the area around Nieuwpoort which formed the local battle front along the IJzer. Note the lack of any coastal development between De Panne and Nieuwpoort. The Vicinal routes shown in lightly checked lines are those that existed when the map was surveyed, apparently late in 1913: only the Oostduinkerke – Veurne – De Panne sections remained operational during the War. The Allied forward area between Veurne and the river had a complex network of 60 cm-gauge supply lines.

3. Urban trams in Oostende and Knokke

3.1 Preface

From 1931 the coastal tramway catered for interurban journeys and the connection of resorts to railway stations. But the system also served, slightly as an afterthought, local needs within two of the towns served, Oostende and Knokke and we will consider these next. The former, with a population of 44,000 in 1930, was by far the largest centre on the route and as well as its many hotels and heavy holiday traffic also contained industrial and port facilities supported by a large working population. Knokke was different, almost entirely a pleasure resort which had grown rapidly from a village sheltering behind the dunes to a major – and by choice notably select – holiday town. Local tram services came later there and were associated with land development.

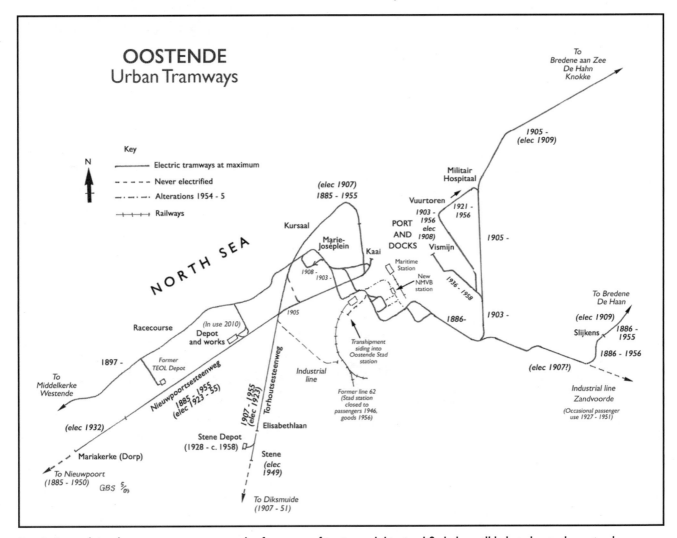

Map 5: Oostende's urban tram system was complex for a town of its size and this simplified plan will help to locate the main places. The purely urban routes all closed in 1955 – 58, and only the through line from top right to centre left survives in 2010.

3.2 Oostende town tramways 1885 – 1958

The map of the town shows the localities mentioned in this section

Oostende was well established long before the tramways arrived, but its enlargement westwards along the Coast called for local transport. The 1885 steam tramway to Nieuwpoort started the urban network because it made its way in an arc along the sea-front around the north-east of the town from its terminus near the Railway Station before heading south-west along the Nieuwpoortsesteenweg. The 1886 Blankenberge line next brought tracks into the town centre from the north-east. The 1897 electric line to Middelkerke also served part of the town, and its operators (TEOL) began a local service in 1896 with a fleet of seven accumulator cars, later extended east over steam tram tracks as far as Slijkens on the Bredene line. The first wholly local branch opened to the north-east side of the harbour in 1903, initially with steam traction and serving the Vuurtoren ('lighthouse') district. The electrification of

Service 4, the penultimate local route to run in Oostende, served the neighbouring village of Slijkens where No 9232 of 1908 was photographed in July 1955. Prominent is the rotatable bow collector (unlike British 'flip-over' collectors) with its 'wind-balance' which helped to maintain contact pressure in gales. This was the route of the 1886 steam tramway towards the north-east via Bredene, later replaced as the main line by the present coastal section. The service was withdrawn in 1956.
[J.Bazin courtesy MUPDOFER]

both routes to De Haan in 1909 extended the wires and made possible electrification of the Vuurtoren line in 1908, lengthened in 1921 to form a large loop via Militair Hospitaal and rejoining the coastal route. Unusually this branch was worked only in the clockwise direction: it carried heavy summer traffic to various holiday sites.

Access to the town centre was improved with the opening of a line between the station and Marie Joséplein in 1903, electrically worked from 1909. A further long-distance line entered the town from Diksmuide along Torhoutsesteenweg in June 1907: this service remained steam, and later autorail (diesel tram), operated until closure in 1951. The accumulator cars were converted to overhead power in 1908 and continued in local service.

There were plans for several urban extensions prior to 1914, but the outbreak of war (when the whole urban network

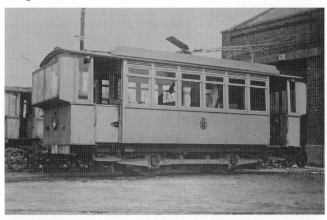

The TEOL's first motor trams of 1896 were adapted by enclosure of their platforms, including a curious 'bay window' extension to clear the brake handle originally fitted outside the dash. No 9171 had been adapted for works service when photographed after the 1940 – 45 War in Oostende depot yard: it was in this form that these trams worked urban services until the 1940s.

Delivery of the fine 'Coast Standard' bogie cars from 1930 freed older two-axle cars for secondary use. No 9249 was built for the OB in 1909 and has been improved by the addition of platform doors to rebuff the coastal breezes. It is seen in fine condition on a typical Oostende urban working in August 1956, at Marie-Joséplein, the terminus of many local services. [National Tramway Museum, M.J. O'Connor]

was closed) ended these, and post-war proposals also came to nothing. After the war the Vicinal followed its practice in several of the towns and cities it served, electrifying the suburban inner sections of its steam-worked interurban lines. In 1923 electric traction began along the 1885 steam line to Nieuwpoort as far as Mariakerke (Ruslandstraat, now Lijsterbeslaan), and the 1907 Diksmuide line as far as Stene (Elisabethlaan). Electric traction was extended outwards on both these routes, in 1932 to Mariakerke (Dorpstraat) and in 1949 to Stene (Hoge Barreel). There were alterations to the town centre layout between the wars, and a further electric branch on the east bank of the harbour opened in 1936, serving the large new fish market or 'Vismijn'.

To house the growing electric fleet a new depot was opened at Stene in 1928, but problems with flooding caused ongoing difficulties. It lasted until about 1958, latterly used for scrapping.

3.3 Knokke

The situation in far smaller Knokke resembled that in Oostende to the extent that the original trunk tramway passed through part of the town (Brugge – Heist, 1890). This was supplemented by the short horse line along what became the main boulevard, taken over by the Vicinal and electrified in 1912. Electric trams from Oostende then ran to the sea front at Van Bunnenplein along the prestigious and elegant Lippenslaan, the tracks running either side of a central reservation later attractively planted with flowers and shrubs. After the First World War the continuing development of the town led to extension along the sea front eastwards, to Oosthoek (Café Siska) in 1928, and beyond to the Dutch frontier at Retranchement in 1929. This opened up a second running connection into the Netherlands over the SBM steam tramway leading to Breskens. Finally an entirely new branch westwards to join the interurban line at Heist, parallel with the Coast and passing the Casino, was opened between 1929 and 1935. This little network provided for a range of local services, mainly operating only during the summer months, between Siska and Heist via the Casino, and between Siska and the main-line railway station (which had opened in 1920).

3.4 Rolling stock on town services

Electric rolling stock is described in chapter 6, but we can note here that services began in Oostende with slightly rebuilt two axled cars inherited from the 1897 Middelkerke line, supported by the accumulator cars rebuilt for overhead electric traction. Beginning in 1932 eight cars were re-bodied in a distinctive, angular, but not unattractive style, and five more were drastically rebuilt in 1947-8 retaining little of the original structure. These thirteen cars handled many urban workings in both Knokke and Oostende to the end, supplemented by 'main-line' cars: even bogie cars were occasionally used. The overall requirements of the two urban networks were small, with running times typically about fifteen minutes per sector and service frequencies

Most of the miscellaneous two-axled cars which operated town services in Oostende and Knokke were rebodied after 1932 in an angular but not displeasing style. No 9098 is seen at the 'Waterhuis' Brasserie on Oostende Kaai in September 1953. This was a tram with a long history, having been built for an independent metre-gauge line in Brussels in 1897, but was radically rebuilt in 1932 with this four-window body. These cars were scrapped by 1955.

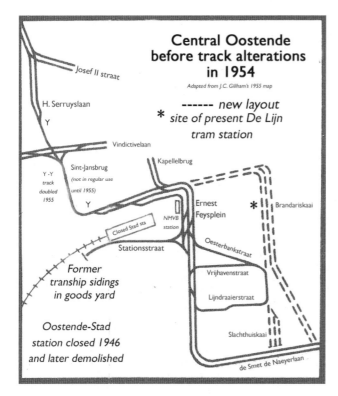

Map 6. The track layout in the south centre of Oostende was drastically altered in 1954-5 with the demolition of the former Stad (town) station and the construction of a new Vicinal station. This diagram adapted from a map by the late John Gillham shows the relationship between the old and new layouts.

of two or three cars an hour. In 1938 a pool of thirty cars was assigned for local services in Oostende and Knokke, but the final timetable for the last urban branch (Oostende service 8 to Vismijn) required only one car for most of the day with two in the morning peak.

3.5 The end of town trams, and rerouting in Oostende

Knokke saw the end of its local services first. The communal council began pressing for the cessation of tramway operation as early as February 1950, justified both by the growth in motor traffic and the congestion alleged to be caused by trams, and by the fact that the sort of affluent visitors the town desired now travelled in their own cars and wanted to park them where they chose. The whole of the local service ended on 30 June 1951, and the Brugge interurban service was withdrawn in 1956. At the end of June 1963 the council banned tram traffic along Lippenslaan for the summer season, tramcars now being thought unsuitable for the elegant surroundings they had helped to foster. This necessitated improvised arrangements to reverse the Oostende trams outside the railway station, requiring a motor luggage-van to shunt the trailers. Although winter operation to Het Zoute was permitted this too ended on 30 June 1966, and a loop was installed at Knokke terminus with a connecting bus onwards.

In Oostende too the council sought to end tram operation but slightly later, in February 1952. The lines to the east of the docks had been closed during the war, but service resumed on the Vuurtoren route in 1948 and to Vismijn in 1949, when major bomb damage to the bridges across the Brugge canal was repaired after use of a lengthy diversionary route. There was even a short electric extension at Stene. The non-electric lines to Nieuwpoort and Diksmuide had ceased operation by 1951, bringing to an end steam and diesel operation on the Coast. With growing political opposition the Vicinal agreed to the abandonment of all the urban lines, following what was becoming Vicinal practice, beginning in Brugge in 1950, to replace minor urban tramways with one-man-operated buses, with pronounced economic benefits. The Stene and Mariakerke routes ended in 1955, Slijkens and Vuurtoren in 1956 (although the latter branch was certainly still wired in 1963 and was used by summer specials serving a childrens' holiday camp), and finally the short Vismijn branch in 1958. All central Oostende tracks apart from the present through route were abandoned.

Meanwhile major urban redevelopment associated with the demolition of the closed town (Stad) station (the former railway route became the inner end of the new Brussels – Oostende motorway) required extensive tramway re-routing, and the central track layout was altered in 1954. The proposals had been drawn up by SELVOP during the war and took account of planned changes in the road pattern and adaptation of older docks for leisure purposes. The plans were approved by the Government in November 1945, but their realisation depended on alterations to the dock walls, removal of massive German wartime installations, and relocation of utilities including a trunk gas main. In post-war conditions these alterations took some years, and by the time they were complete the urban network was already doomed.

The new route was 360m shorter than the old and eliminated several awkward road crossings, as well as introducing level and convenient interchange between ferries, main-line trains, and trams. An entirely new NMVB/SNCV station was built at Brandariskaai closer to the Maritime station. This was later greatly enlarged into its present form.

New storage sidings were built at Slachthuiskaai adjoining the new station, and a new turning loop laid in side streets nearby. The long-established depot and works in Nieuwpoortsesteenweg remained in use, after 1967 reached over a single track in Spoortstraat, although most operations now take place from a base in the enlarged station sidings.

4. *SELVOP* and the completion of the coastal chain 1927 – 1955

4.1 Preface

Following financial restructuring by *RELSE* the operating contract was reassigned from 22 April 1927 for the remainder of the lease to a new affiliate, *La Société pour l'Exploitation des Lignes Vicinales d'Ostende et des Plages Belges* ('*SELVOP*'), or *Maatschappij voor Exploitatie van de Buurtspoorwegen van Oostende en de Belgische Badplaatsen* ('*MEBOBB*'). The new management faced the major task of extending electrification over the network, providing the rolling stock needed to resource a larger system, and upgrading the older sections of the main line. It is worth reflecting briefly on the state of coastal development by the 1920s. Although De Panne, Nieuwpoort, Oostende and Blankenberge were now well-established resorts, and Knokke had developed greatly since 1900, elsewhere settlement was still patchy.

There was no continuous coastal road south-west of Nieuwpoort (Bad) and little building between Zeebrugge and Blankenberge. Although the dunes were being afforested with willow and pine to stabilise them much remained to be done, and communities such as De Haan were still little more than villages with a scattering of villas. The Coast was still largely a select, affluent holiday area and it is significant that two classes of travel were catered for on many coastal trams until 1947.

It is also relevant to note in this context that *RELSE* and *SELVOP* were subsidiaries of a multi-national financial and industrial

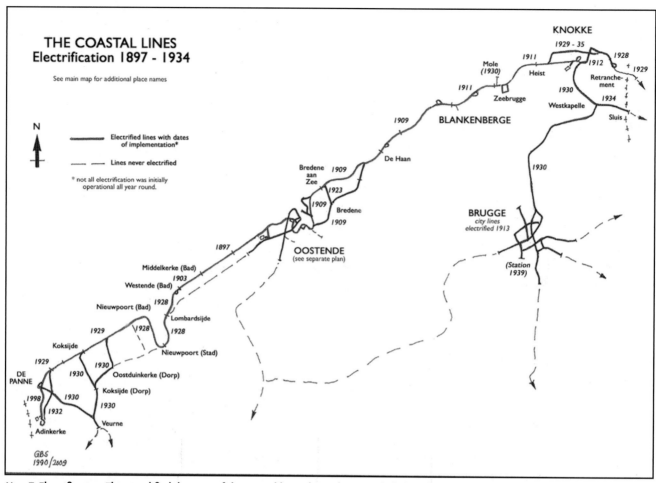

Map 7. Electrification. This simplified diagram of the coastal lines shows the spread of electrification from 1897 to 1934.

empire headed by the fascinating and enigmatic banker and entrepreneur Édouard Empain (ennobled as Baron Empain in 1907). An important aspect of Empain's work involved property and estate development, notably in Egypt where his *Cairo Electric Railways and Heliopolis Oases Company* created from 1906 a new and select settlement in the desert near Cairo, a development made possible by construction of a high-quality electric railway link across the sands (Empain's lavish Heliopolis Palace Hotel is now the residence of Egypt's President). The parallel with the exploitation of the Belgian Coast is interesting.

4.2 Electrification completed
The progress of electrification is shown on map 7.
Post-war the first task, which began before *SELVOP*'s birth, was to restore damaged and destroyed lines and then to resume the expansion plans which came to a summary end in 1914. Routes around Nieuwpoort, the worst-damaged area, were reinstated by 1920, although destroyed canal bridges required temporary structures for several years. Subsequent changes greatly altered the tramway scene. In 1926 the branch from Nieuwpoort (Stad) to the seaside was extended along the Coast, joining

The 1890 steam tramway between Knokke and Brugge was electrified in 1930, and just before the Second World War its Brugge terminus was extended to serve the fine new railway station. In April 1954 'Coast Standard' No 9953 stands on the terminal loop: by then this was the only tramway in Brugge, and it lasted another two years. Notice the number 'plaque' on the dash (for Brugge – Het Zoute service 10), and the 'coastal' heavy-duty pantograph with dual contact strips.
[Tony Percival]

The last major extension of the Coast Line until recently was the branch from De Panne to Adinkerke railway station (now named 'De Panne'). This 1932 line entered the station forecourt from the opposite direction to the present route, terminating in front of the imposing station building whose shadow can be seen on the ground. In August 1956 ex-OB motor No 9476 of 1911 is ready to leave for De Panne at the head of a pair of ex-steam two-axled trailers (Nos 1654 and 1876). The tram has been slightly modified, notably by the addition of platform doors. The line had operated only intermittently since early 1955 and was closed later in 1956. The present Adinkerke terminus, opened in 1998, is to the left of the picture, approached from the far right distance.
[National Tramway Museum, M.J. O'Connor]

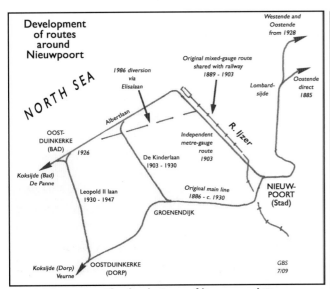

Map 8. Nieuwpoort. The development of lines around Nieuwpoort is complicated and this diagram will help to explain the sequence.

This advertisement for the arduous through connection between Oostende and Walcheren appeared in SELVOP's 1936 timetable (but has been partly reset to overcome faults in the original). Note that the Netherlands did not then subscribe to the International Meridian and hence, as shown here, Dutch time varied by twenty minutes from Belgian time which had been aligned with Greenwich mean time since 1892. This changed in 1940.

at Koksijde (Bad) the restored 1914 line onwards to De Panne: all this was initially steam-worked. In 1928 the 1897 Oostende – Westende line was also completed as long intended, when electric cars began running via Lombardsijde to Nieuwpoort, but wires were still not complete beyond. During 1928 through electric trams from Oostende were hauled by steam locomotives beyond Nieuwpoort until electrification was finished throughout the following year. Isolated amidst the growing sea of electrification the original inland line from Oostende as far as Nieuwpoort (Stad) remained steam operated, mainly for goods traffic. In 1930 the original 1903 spur between Groenendijk and Nieuwpoort (Bad) was lifted and a new single track electrified connection opened directly between Oostduinkerke (Dorp) and the seaside. The original main line between Nieuwpoort (Stad) and Oostduinkerke (Dorp) was never electrified and was eventually abandoned. (Map 8 helps to explain these complications).

Enhancement of the coastal lines proceeded with impressive speed. In the initial post-war optimism the plan for an international link to Dunkerque was revived, but eventually foundered in the hostile financial conditions after 1929, the French metre gauge line serving Bray Dunes, which it would have joined, having already closed to passengers. Had the link been built it would have created maybe the only tramway in the world to serve three nations on a single route because in 1929 another electrified extension had been opened at the far eastern end of the Coast, between Het Zoute and the Dutch town of Retranchement. Here the Vicinal line connected with the Dutch SBM steam tramway, to which it was already linked at Sluis and Aardenburg, and through trains

At the western extremity of its route the Coast Line passed through the narrow main street of De Panne, as it still does today. In a view typical of the inter-war years an ex-OB motor with two-axled trailers in tow is turning off the main line into Zeelaan towards Adinkerke in 1937. The service number '14' (as the route was then designated) can just be made out on the original card.

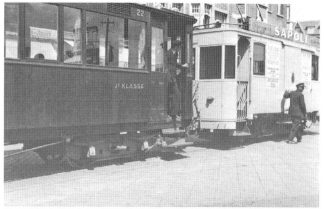

There are not many views of the through carriages which ran between the Dutch SBM tramway and the Vicinal, changing between steam and electric traction at Sluis or Retranchement. In this 1930s view one of the Franco-Belge motor luggage vans (Nos 9950 – 9954 and 9965 – 9966 built in 1909-11) is coupled to a varnished SBM bogie trailer at Knokke. Similar trailer No 24 of 1925 has been preserved at Hoorn in the Netherlands.

between Breskens and Knokke operated over the route, changing between steam and electric traction at Retranchement. This new line facilitated one of the most adventurous tramway rides in Europe, offering through bookings between Oostende and the Dutch town of Middelburg on the Island of Walcheren, involving both electric and steam trams, a ferry, and a Dutch train, taking three hours from Oostende. The service operated on summer Thursdays (Middelburg market days) until 1939.

In 1923 a short spur from the Coast serving the new Bredene racecourse was brought into use.

Electric traction was extended in 1930 to Veurne from both Koksijde (Dorp) and De Panne. The line between Brugge and Knokke was also electrified in 1930, and the branch from Westkappelle to Sluis followed in 1934. Part of the Brugge route was relocated along a new road in 1936, requiring alterations at Knokke railway station. The Dutch section of the Sluis branch beyond the Anna ter Muiden border post remained in the ownership of the connecting SBM company, but the electrical equipment was owned by the Vicinal. Along the coastal main line sections previously built as rural single-lines were all doubled by 1940 although the branches remained largely single.

In the course of reconstructing the main line, and electrifying some of the extensions, catenary overhead was used in places, the first on the Vicinal and using distinctive bracket arms.

The development of Anglo-Belgian passenger steamer services at Zeebrugge led to the building of a maritime terminal on the Mole, served by an electrified branch which opened in 1930. Special trams ran to coastal destinations in connection with steamers.

Meanwhile at the other end of the Coast a new electric line, replacing the 60 cm gauge tramway, was opened in 1932 from De Panne to Adinkerke, so that a continuous chain of electric tramways reached from Brugge and Het Zoute to De Panne, Veurne, and Adinkerke, a total route length of some 150 km. Through electric operation between De Panne and Knokke-Het Zoute had commenced in September 1931, but Baron Empain did not live to see this fulfilment as he had died in Brussels in 1929.

'The man who made the Coast': Baron Édouard Empain whose companies controlled the coastal tramways for over half a century.

The following table summarises the complex creation of the present coastal route.

4.3 Operation

SELVOP had a difficult task in operating its greatly-expanded electric empire, and, as described in chapter 6, relied initially on a somewhat heterogeneous fleet of mainly four-wheeled trams and trailers inherited from pre-1914 operations, and gathered from across the Vicinal network, supplemented by some newly-built cars, including a few bogie motors. Overall the quality and performance of these trams fell short of what was required for relatively long-distance travel and to meet the expectations of a discerning and affluent clientele. The resourcing of a new fleet was not helped by the disastrous consequences of the Wall Street Crash of October 1929, which suddenly cut off sources of finance (Belgium's national income fell by over 25 per cent between 1930 and 1932 and had not fully recovered by the outbreak of war). It seems possible that otherwise a larger new

Section	Year
Knokke – Heist	1890
Heist – Blankenberge	1908
Blankenberge – De Haan Junction	1886
De Haan Junction – Rederijkaai	1905
Rederijkaai – Slijkensesteenweg	1903
Route through Oostende	1886 - 1903
Diversion via Brandariskaai (new NMVB station)	1954
Oostende – Middelkerke (Bad)	1897
Middelkerke (Bad) – Westende (Bad)	1903
Westende (Bad) – Lombardsijde	1928
Lombardsijde – Nieuwpoort (Stad)	1885
Nieuwpoort (Stad) – (Bad) (NMVB line)	1903
Nieuwpoort (Bad) – Koksijde (Bad)	1926
Diversion in Nieuwpoort via Elisalaan	1986
Koksijde (Bad) – De Panne	1914/1920
[De Panne – Adinkerke (De Panne Station)	1998]

The Coast Standard tram in all its glory: this is a post-war view at Heist (note the modern bogie trailer) but No 10052 is in virtually original condition. Notice the heavy riveted underframe, (which lasted over fifty years and was later used under an SO motor), the two-tone warning horns on the roof, the number plaque on the dash, and the side route board. On the left hand side of the cab roof is the illuminated display box for the service number, a device only briefly used: because through cars between Knokke and De Panne changed number at Oostende it was impracticable to use this system without a ladder and delay and they were swiftly discontinued.

fleet would have been built, and in particular that more would have been done to replace the older trailer cars, some dating back to the steam era. As it was, fourteen newly-built trailers, matching the new motor trams, were withdrawn in 1932 to be converted into motors themselves, thus completing the fleet more economically but requiring continued use of existing two-axled trailers. The Coast Line achieved its maximum rolling-stock complement in 1935, with 121 motors and 147 trailers.

With this, and the electric network complete, it is timely to look at services in the high season of 1935 (13 July – 2 September). On the 'main line' De Panne – Oostende was served by two cars an hour with extras, mostly running through to and from Knokke. The Oostende – Knokke – Het Zoute service was generally more frequent with up to six cars an hour in each direction. Brugge - Het Zoute had 32 round trips daily, i.e. about two cars an hour, with twenty between Sluis and Westkappelle, about half of which ran through to and from Knokke. There were eight round trips between Knokke and Retranchement. The sections Veurne – Koksijde (Dorp) – Koksijde (Bad), Veurne – De Panne, and Adinkerke – De Panne each had about twenty round trips daily. The 'inland' route Oostende – Bredene (Dorp) – De Haan had nine journeys each way, and Veurne – Koksijde (Dorp) – Oostduinkerke (Dorp) and (Bad) six round trips, with seven extras in the afternoon between Koksijde (Dorp) and (Oostduinkerke (Bad) only. Non-electrified Oostende – Diksmuide had seven return journeys, plus one each way running Brugge – Leke – Oostende. Lastly, the original Oostende – Nieuwpoort – Veurne section by now had only a single weekly steam train, on Wednesdays: the rest of this service was worked by bus.

Destinations and intermediate points were originally displayed on long side boards at cantrail level, rather like those once seen on British trains. Service numbers took the form of coloured 'plaques' on the dash. The numbers were changed from time to time and there was a major post-war revision, but the following are those published by *SELVOP* in 1936. The illustrations show the general style of the displays, and apart from a brief period on some rebuilt cars in the early 1930s there were no roller blind indicators on the Coast until the 1950s.

No	Route
1	Oostende – Het Zoute
1D	Oostende – De Haan via Bredene Village
2	Oostende – De Panne
2D	Oostende – Westende Bad
3	Oostende – Vuurtoren
4	Oostende – Slijkens
5	Town service: see below
6	Town service: see below
7	Koksijde (Bad) – Veurne
8	De Panne – Veurne
9	Oostduinkerke Bad – Veurne
10	Brugge – Het Zoute
12	Heist – Oosthoek (Siska)
14	De Panne – Adinkerke
21	Knokke – Sluis

Oostende town services 5 and 6 followed a complex 8.5km circular itinerary crossing over itself at Petit Paris. In 1936 Service 5 ran Mariakerke (Bad) – Kaai Station – Kursaal – Stene (Elisabethlaan), service 6 the same itinerary but starting and finishing further along Nieuwpoortsesteenweg at Mariakerke (Dorp).

The two sectors of the main line, either side of Oostende, were separately numbered 1 and 2: however in practice many services ran from end to end, changing number on the approaches to Oostende.

4.4 War again

The Second World War (1939-45) had a considerable impact on the coastal system and damage was widespread, but the strategic background was relatively simple. The Germans invaded Belgium on 9/10 May 1940 and the King surrendered on 28 May after nearly 24,000 Belgian troops had been killed or injured and the British had been compelled to evacuate their army from the Continent. In the course of the British retreat to the beaches close to the French frontier that end of the tramway again found itself under German attack, especially around De Panne which was shelled and bombed in late May 1940 leading to the withdrawal of tram services for a month. The whole of Belgium was occupied and placed under military rule, and the Coast was again heavily fortified against Allied invasion, becoming the most strongly-defended major coastline in the world: no successful seaborne landing ever occurred here. Incidentally the Départements of Nord and Pas-de-Calais adjoining the border were detached from French jurisdiction altogether and placed under the control of the German High Command in Brussels.

The building of German coastal defence batteries caused local disruption to tram operation near Oostende and the urban lines into the east bank port area were again closed. Special measures were necessary for trams on the main line to pass through sections where overhead lines were removed to free fields of fire. By early 1943 the overhead lines were removed over the longer coastal stretch between Mariakerke (Bad) and Middelkerke (Bad) and although initially trains were hauled by steam locomotives through the affected area the coastal line was closed completely at the end of 1943 and all trains reverted to steam haulage via the inland route to Nieuwpoort (Stad). The coastal route was partly dismantled to facilitate construction of the Germans' 'Atlantic Wall', remains of which may still be seen south-west of Oostende, and the line was not fully reinstated until 1946.

Because traffic had fallen considerably, and because it was considered prudent to remove the best rolling stock from an area subject to bombardment, most of the relatively new 'standard' motors, as well as many trailers, were withdrawn from the Coast in 1940 and redeployed or stored in Brussels and elsewhere. They made their way by successive Vicinal lines via Gent and Asse, albeit hauled by steam locomotives, the through journey taking up to five days. 29 of the 35 standards were evacuated in this way. A few were recalled in 1941-2, required for extra services to carry workers on the fortifications decreed by Hitler late in 1941: 26 had returned by 1944 (three had been destroyed in 1943).

A major value of Belgium to the Germans was the availability of level land for military airfields from which to conduct bombing operations against Great Britain. Construction and enlargement of Luftwaffe facilities caused three tramways to close: Koksijde – Veurne in 1941; Koksijde (Dorp) – (Bad), and Oostduinkerke (Dorp) – (Bad) in 1944. The Veurne branch never reopened (the Belgian Air Component (COMOPSAIR) airfield still extends over the track bed), but although the other lines resumed operation after 1945 strong opposition to tram operation by the communal authorities in Koksijde brought service over the loop to an end again in 1947. In the north-east Knokke (Bunnenplein) – Siska was closed in 1943 but reopened in 1945, but the extension into the Netherlands at Retranchement was closed at the outbreak of war and later lifted. Post-war proposals by the SBM for reinstatement and electrification to Breskens came to nothing, although a 'Coast Standard' tram was displayed in the Netherlands in 1947 to show what could have been.

Allied bombing as well as sabotage by the Resistance had damaged or destroyed bridges at Nieuwpoort, Oostende, Zeebrugge, and Heist, and there was further bomb damage including to the depot at Knokke, and the traction substation at Blankenberge. Canadian and Belgian troops liberated the coastal region as far as Oostende, reached on 9 September 1944, but German defence of the Scheldt bridgehead, with prolonged and heavy fighting around Breskens, meant that the eastern end of the line from Zeebrugge to Knokke was not liberated until 3 November 1944. As a result all tramways in the north-east were closed from September 1944 until early 1945. Several sections of the tramway, notably at Nieuwpoort, Oostende, and Zeebrugge, were destroyed for the second time in thirty years.

4.5 Post-war optimism, and reality

Given the scale of destruction, especially at the eastern end of the line, it is remarkable that the system was restored by 1946, and in the summer of 1947 a service was offered roughly hourly the length of the line. There were 17 through departures from Oostende to Het Zoute between 06.02 and 20.41, half the service running via the Coast out of Oostende and half via Bredene village. Running time was 76 minutes (81 via the village). An additional morning and evening

This expressive view perfectly evokes the post-war atmosphere. It was taken in April 1954 opposite the old town station, and shows one of the three newer baggage-motors (No 10020 of 1932, still extant) with an eastbound train of elderly and varied balcony trailers and a luggage van. These tracks were abandoned in 1954 but the present tramway runs across the scene in the background. [Tony Percival]

This page from the Vicinal's 1947 timetable shows the limited service offered that summer. Notice that some workings are routed via the inland line between Nieuwpoort and Koksijde soon to be closed.

Another of Tony Percival's evocative views at the Kaai in 1954 captures the spirit of a slightly down-at-heel coastal train of that era, hauled by a luggage-motor and attended by the juveniles of Oostende. [Tony Percival]

Vicinal good wagons were not often photographed. This varied and down-at-heel rake was stabled in the storage sidings alongside Slijkensesteenweg east of Oostende in September 1957. Public goods traffic had ceased five years earlier. [Tony Percival]

shuttle service between Oostende and Bredene-aan-Zee catered for local traffic. From Oostende to De Panne there were also 17 through departures between 05.15 and 20.40, eight of which ran via the inland loop through Koksijde (Dorp). Running time was 71 minutes (84 via the village loop). This service was markedly less than that offered in 1935, reflecting pressures on power and rolling stock, and damage to the route. For several years after the war pending full restoration of destroyed road bridges at Oostende, Nieuwpoort, and Zeebrugge mixed gauge track was laid over neighbouring railway bridges, shared by NMVB/SNCV and National Railways trains.

An event with important, if not wholly successful, consequences for the Vicinal occurred in August 1948 when an American-built single-ended 'PCC' tram arrived on the Coast for trials, sponsored by the Belgian engineering company ACEC. (The PCCs were groundbreaking American city cars developed from first principles by the US Electric Railway Presidents' Conference Committee, and introduced in North American cities from 1936). The car had been built by the St Louis Car Company in 1947 and shipped complete to Europe, initially for trials in Brussels. On the Coast, numbered 10419 by the Vicinal and mounted on metre-gauge American-built trucks, it ran on test and in service on circular urban lines around Knokke and Oostende, and from July 1949 operated regularly between Oostende and Westende at weekends. It even made a test trip to Brugge. Although 10419's size, style, and modern interior pleased passengers its performance was less satisfactory. The bogies were unsuited to the relatively light rail of the Coast line, its potential speed was impracticable, whilst its electrical consumption was forty per cent higher than a standard car's. 10419 left Oostende in October 1949, but it evidently impressed the Vicinal as they ordered 24 Belgian-built and narrower trams of the same basic design in 1950, although these never came to the Coast. These trials are one of the interesting 'what ifs?' of the coastal history: had circumstances been more favourable there might have been a very different fleet, and indeed the single-ended configuration of 10419 was adopted for the 'SO' rebuilds

The imported American PCC car, numbered 10419 by the Vicinal, ran on the coast, on test and in service, for fourteen months in 1948-9, but no production models were ever used there. It is seen here in Oostende: notice how the full-width body overhangs the Clark B3-type metre-gauge trucks.

During the 1950s track-lifting was prevalent along the coastal system: this view in March 1959 shows track being removed from the outer boulevard in Brugge. (The photographer –GS– lived nearby and grieved).

a few years later. By the 1950s the origin of the Vicinal lines around Oostende as agricultural light railways was increasingly irrelevant, although goods traffic had been vital during the war years. The goods-only section of the first steam line out of Oostende, to Nieuwpoort via the inland route, where traffic had dwindled almost to nothing, was finally closed in 1951.

Over the rest of the coastal network the resumption of road transport after the war speedily reduced goods by rail: in the whole year 1949-50 only 1,315 wagon loads were handled, mainly of coal and building material via Oostende, and it is unsurprising that goods traffic ended in 1952. This was not all. Faced with the inexorable rise in costs and steady fall in traffic the concessionaires had little alternative except to propose a steady series of peripheral closures, to which the Vicinal and the provincial authorities necessarily agreed. By the end of 1958 the coastal tramway had contracted to its main core.

4.6 *SELVOP* expires

By 1955 the commercially lucrative years of the tramway in Belgium were long past and *SELVOP*'s controlling interests were developing activities elsewhere. Their tramways in Liège and Charleroi were also facing decline and the Vicinal was no longer granting operating concessions, so the expiry of their lease on 31 December 1955 brought *SELVOP*'s tumultuous era to an end.

They had valiantly battled to restore the tramway to full operation after the destruction of 1940-44 and it is a remarkable testimony that all but two sections did resume operation in 1945-6 although three others closed again shortly afterwards, amidst local acrimony. The hostility of local authorities also condemned local tramway operation in Oostende and Knokke, and the Sluis and Brugge lines had closed. However the fact that the returning holiday crowds were handled with aplomb from 1947 is a testimony to the company and their loyal staff.

SELVOP's longer-lived legacy included the 'Coast Standard' trams and the completed double-line route. The Vicinal assumed direct operation of the Coast lines on 1 January 1956.

For convenience a list of closures is given in the table below.

Closure of branch and local lines 1947-58

Year	Section	Remarks
1947	Oostduinkerke (Dorp) – (Bad)	Reopened post-war
	Koksijde (Dorp) – (Bad)	Reopened post-war
	Oostduinkerke (Dorp) - Koksijde (Dorp)	Reopened post-war
1950	Most Brugge local lines	
1951	Oostende (Mariakerke) – Nieuwpoort (Stad)	Steam: goods only post-war
	Oostende (Stene) – Diksmuide	Not electric
	Westkapelle – Sluis	
	Urban lines in Knokke	
	Brugge (Station) - Markt	
1953	Veurne - Ieper	Not electric
	Veurne – Poperinge	Not electric
1954	De Panne – Veurne	
1955	Oostende – Stene	
	Oostende – Mariakerke	
	Oostende town centre lines	
	Slijkens – Bredene - De Haan (Sous-station)	'Villages' loop
1956	Brugge – Knokke	
	Oostende - Slijkens	Stub of 'villages' loop
	Oostende – Vuurtoren	Special cars until c 1963
	Adinkerke – De Panne	
1958	Oostende - Vismijn	Last local line

Acknowledgements for chronological data to; Nos Vicinaux, Vancraeynest (1986); Dieudonné (1987); and Davies (2006) (see bibliography).

5. 'Threats and opportunities': revival, the end of the Vicinal, and the coming of *De Lijn* 1956–2008

5.1 Preface

The Vicinal's repossession of the coastal tramway on 1 January 1956 has been described as a re-awakening, as the greater resources of a larger organisation became available, but such optimism hid some ominous facts. The Vicinal rail system was already in decline: the total route length had fallen from 4,236 km in 1950 to 2,505 in 1955, and even the electrified length had begun to shrink from its maximum (1511 km in 1952). The number of electric trams had fallen from 1,003 in 1950 to 812 in 1955. The familiar post-war phenomenon of rising labour costs in a booming industrial economy, unmatched by rising fare income, threatened the Vicinal's financial stability, and it remained solvent only by introducing motor-bus operation in place of rail. Finally the whole coastal route, although restored after 1945 and maintained in reasonable condition, required major investment to equip it for the future: the track was not fully ballasted and had never been wholly stable, with wind-blown sand a persistently

The new Oostende Vicinal station included storage sidings at Slachthuiskaai, now a large maintenance area. In early 1956 this was the somewhat untidy scene two years after the track diversion had been completed. One of the 1932 motor luggage-vans is shunting an elderly two-axled trailer (No 11582 of 1909). The new 1954 line towards Knokke ascends the ramp on the left, whilst the original main line ran along the raised roadway in the right background. The back-street turning loop diverges to the right. [National Tramway Museum, H.B. Priestley]

damaging feature; and the wind and salt-laden atmosphere attacked overhead line equipment. The Vicinal would address these problems, but the closure programme begun in 1951 was continued.

As described in chapter 3, the major road alterations in Oostende which followed the demolition of the now disused Stad station led to important changes to the tramway layout in the town. New storage sidings and a handsome station building were provided for the Vicinal, and the whole ensemble gave a good introduction to the Coast Line. These works were completed in June 1954.

5.2 The SO-series and threats to the future

The first and rapid manifestation of the new regime was the re-bodying of most of the 1930-32 'standards' in modern style, forming the 28 'SO' single-ended motors delivered in 1956-7. These are described fully in Chapter 6, but it is worth noting that resources did not extend to wholly new vehicles: the running gear and equipment of the SOs were already over twenty years old. The Vicinal later showed both imagination and prudence in providing new trailers derived from surplus N-type motors, but throughout the 1960s the fleet remained heterogeneous and some older trailers remained in peak season service.

It is interesting briefly to overview Coast operations after delivery of all 28 SO motors, which revived the coastal network. The NMVB/SNCV timetable for the summer of 1957 shows 30 through daily departures from Oostende and Het Zoute between 05.10 and 00.30, with a high season running time of 71 minutes. Departures were generally every thirty minutes with extras. Between Oostende and De Panne there were 25 through departures between 05.07 and 23.27, with a running time of 71 minutes. Trams ran every half hour, and most workings ran through between Het Zoute and De Panne. These running times

New Vicinal trams were once delivered by rail, or even over the undertaking's own linked tracks. In 1956 when the first 'SO' series cars were ready a massive road assemblage was used and No 10045 –the third car built– is seen awaiting despatch on 24 March 1956 from its birthplace, the Rue Eloy works in Cureghem, Brussels. This shows the sleek off-side of these single-ended trams. The 25 m-long road tractor AT 553 was built in 1954 and used a 150 hp Brossel diesel engine.

The single-ended SO motors had a 'train door' at the rear to facilitate ticket collection en route, and were also equipped with back-up control and brake equipment for reversing moves and for use in emergency. This view of 10045 shows the air brake on the right and the controller (without handle) on the left. The rear of the SOs had five windows, the ends of the 'NO' trailers three.

This slightly blurred view gives a fine impression of a 1960s train at speed, with SO motor No 9819 racing through the dunes beneath typical Vicinal catenary overhead, and with two post-war trailers behind (distinguished from the standards by their flatter roofs and different windows).

At its south-western end in Knokke the Coast Line originally terminated in a long single-line loop near the sea, until a new circle was built at Esplanade in the 1970s. In this April 1957 view SO motor No 10046 heads two post-war trailers. These views typify train formations early in the history of the SO motors when they worked with older bogie trailers.
[National Tramway Museum, M.J. O'Connor]

show little change from those of 1947 but frequency had doubled and the operating day was much longer. That summer the entire Coast operation required thirty units, including racecourse, special party, and extra trains: the new trams met the 19-train requirement of the base De Panne -Knokke service, working with standard trailers, soon to be supplemented by the ex-'N' trailers, with trains of up to four cars in length. SO's also worked other limited stop and extra trains, with four as a maintenance reserve. Five 'OB' two-axled cars remained in service to cover three workings, including the only surviving branch, to Vismijn in Oostende. No fewer than 85 trailers remained theoretically available for traffic, made up of 30 standards, 4 'Oran' bogies, 6 'Bogota' bogies, and ex-steam bogies 1800 and 1801. The remaining 43 trailers were two-axled, of which 20 were maintained for extra workings, the remainder being in reserve.

Whilst events in Belgium never fully followed their disastrous course in France and Great Britain, where tramways were practically eliminated, the country was not immune to anti-tram pressures: a straw in the wind was the end of tramway operation in the city of Liège in 1967, including the ill-judged closure of *RELSE's* fine Liège – Seraing line. The huge growth in private motor traffic, encouraged by motorway access, and by large-scale building development, confronted the coastal tramway with new problems. The local lines in Knokke had already closed in 1951, and in 1963 the communal council there banned all tramway traffic through the town centre in the high season, ending it altogether in 1967. South-west of Nieuwpoort (Bad) the main road through the string of seaside towns which the tramway had created was now heavily congested and the trams – some on street track in relatively narrow roads – were blamed. In 1968 the Mayor of Nieuwpoort joined his colleagues from other western communes in calling for the removal of the tramways from their streets, impractically calling for their replacement by an elevated monorail. This might have meant the end of the tramway but a number of factors acted in its favour. The principal one was the imbalance between summer and winter traffic (at least four times the number of passengers used the line in August as did in January) which favoured rail operation with motors and trailers, minimising labour requirements whilst using older vehicles at modest continuing cost. With the vehicle technology of the period it would have required a large fleet of new buses (and staff) to handle the same traffic, not a lucrative investment for the short high season. A second positive factor was the amount of reserved track, demonstrating that the tramway was to an extent unaffected by traffic congestion.

Decisively, the Coast was able to benefit from relatively generous central government funding, which also led to investment in underground tramways in Antwerpen from 1975 and the 'light metro' in Charleroi from 1976. The subsequent decline in national prosperity led to the truncation of these schemes: the tram tunnels built in Antwerpen have not all been brought into use and the Charleroi metro was never completed; a similar project in Liège was abandoned and tunnels built there remain unused. The Coast refurbishment was the only one of these 1970s projects outside Brussels to be carried through to completion, a fine memorial to the Vicinal.

At the other end of the line the Vicinal terminus in Het Zoute remained in use during the off-seasons until 1966. In this 1964 view SO motor No 10043 is seen on a special working at the terminal loop in Albertplein. The Vicinal office and shelter are on the right.
[LRTA, Jack Wyse]

The arrival of the SO motors, and the closure of branch lines, finally displaced the elderly 'OB' motors. Heavily-laden No 9234 (built 1908) is seen at the new Vicinal station in Oostende in May 1955 en route for Slijkens, the penultimate Oostende local line to survive.
[LRTA, Jack Wyse]

The Coast in Colour

A view which captures the seaside character of the 1896 electric line between Oostende and Middelkerke: 'SO'-type motor No 10043 and a standard trailer pass Raversijde in September 1964. [LRTA, Jack Wyse]

Over twenty years later a new generation of trams served the Coast: in July 1986 a single-ended BN-type tram in Vicinal livery passes Raversijde. The track and overhead line had both been wholly renewed, the latter with heavy-duty catenary. Beautiful on summer days, but during winter storms single-line working on the landward track is sometimes necessary. [John Bromley]

A further twenty years had produced a third generation of trams: No 6051, one of the 'loaned' Siemens low-floor cars from Antwerpen, works the Oostende – Westende shuttle. On the extreme right can be seen remains of German defence works from the Second World War which caused closure of this section of line in 1943 - 6.

In an early colour view cross-bench car 9998 of 1899 stands at the Brasserie Waterhuis on Oostende Kaai in September 1951. These cars ran almost unchanged for nearly sixty years. [LRTA, Jack Wyse]

There are few colour pictures of Vicinal 'autorails' or diesel trams operating on the coastal network. This is AR 253, one a standard series of over a hundred diesel-engined two-axled cars built in the 1930s, standing outside Veurne railway station in July 1952. It is working the Ieper service which was withdrawn in 1953. In the background a solo 'OB' motor works the electrified service between De Panne and Veurne. [LRTA, Jack Wyse]

This view of No 9513 in the depot yard at Oostende in 1952 shows off the 'SELVOP' period livery with its pale blue stripe, and also the coloured dash 'plaque' and the side route board indicating an Oostende – Westende shuttle. The car dates from 1918 and came to the Coast in 1928, to be rebuilt in this style resembling the 'OB'-type motors. [LRTA, Jack Wyse]

The original luggage-motors ('fourgons- moteurs'), effectively small electric locomotives, were invaluable in shunting, works service, for goods traffic, and to haul long special trains of trailers. No 9954 of 1909 was photographed at Oostende depot in July 1952 attached to an ex-steam traction two-axled trailer. [LRTA, Jack Wyse]

No 9471 was standing in the nearly new Oostende Vicinal station in the summer of 1954, the smart station building (later enlarged) visible in the background. This was one of the last batch of 'OB' motors, built in 1911. In the far distance the main line rises up the new ramp to join the original route by the bridge. [LRTA, Frank Hunt]

Few colour pictures are known of the last branch to be added to the Coast Line, the 800 metre-long route to Vismijn ('Fish Market') in Oostende opened in 1936. The vast market itself can be seen behind No 9476 of 1911 at the terminus. The single-line branch ran partly on reserved track. This was the last urban route on the coast and was abandoned in 1958. [LRTA, MJL]

A damaged picture but worth including as a rare colour view of one of the re-bodied town cars used in Oostende and Knokke. This is No 9111 at the Waterhuis, Oostende in September 1951, one of the four 1897 cars from the Brussels – Boondael line transferred to Oostende in 1928 and later rebuilt in this boxy style. [LRTA, Jack Wyse]

There were once several highly characterful stations along the coast reflecting the rather 'gingerbread' style favoured in Belgium in the early twentieth century. The sole survivor is the eclectic structure at De Haan built at the behest of the King in 1905. SO No 10045 heads towards Knokke in September 1967. [Tony Percival]

In this 1984 view looking towards Knokke BN No 6047 calls on a westbound service. Notice the French version of the station name on the gable end. By this date the building contained a Belgian Railways ticket agency.

The village of De Haan mercifully retains much of its traditional character as this 2005 view shows. BN No 6019 is heading for Knokke, with its rather ugly low-floor centre section clearly visible. The main station building is now a tourist information centre.

In 1984 belated delivery of the fifty single-ended 'Coast' BN-type trams was almost complete, and all but a handful of the double-ended 'Charleroi' version had departed for their eventual home. The storage sidings near Oostende station had been enlarged to contain the new fleet.

By July 2005 the Oostende station storage area had been greatly enlarged and remodelled to serve as the main day-to-day operating base, with a small inspection and repair shed. Siemens car No 6051 working on the shuttle from Westende has just completed its side-street tour round the turning loop (the motorised indicator blind is being turned).

BN-type sets worked briefly in multiple in the 1980s, and in July 1982 a 'Charleroi' double-ended car leads a set into Oostende station from De Panne. Since 1954 the tramway has run alongside the former inner harbour on the right, now a yacht marina with the masts of the Belgian training ship 'Mercator' visible in the background. The old Stad station, seen in earlier views, stood in the far left background.

Oostende station viewed towards De Panne in 1982 with a BN set in multiple unit operation on the left. In the centre is a standard trailer.

Oostende station has changed greatly since it was built in 1954. In July 1982 three different types of tram were in regular service, and the overhead line had been completely replaced. The left hand car in this view is No 6133, one of the double-ended cars working on the Coast between March 1982 and June 1983. In the centre is one of the few remaining SO-motors then still at work.

By the 1990s Oostende station had been transformed again, with a large access bridge and staff accommodation, also serving the adjoining bus station. One unchanged feature: the early twentieth-century Maritime station still stands in the right background (and is to be incorporated into the forthcoming remodelling of the whole complex). In this July 2005 view three BN-type cars are at the platforms: the right hand unit retains its rear coupler and the centre one has a re-constructed cab end incorporating air-conditioning.

Understandably most Coast Line views feature summer scenes, but the trams run throughout the year and 13 December 1998 was a chilly day with a BN-type car in advertising livery at Oostende heading for Knokke.

A street close to Knokke station is happily named 'Tram Way' and its sign commemorates the 1890 steam tramway.

There was an astonishing number of tramcar builders in Belgium: Baume & Marpent were one of about fifteen different manufacturers represented on the Coast alone and this was their decorative builder's plate.

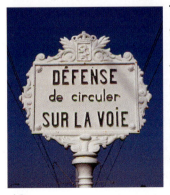

The Vicinal used standard warning signs ('do not walk on the tracks') throughout their system, with the two national languages on either side. This sign has been preserved to add to the historic ambience of De Haan station.

Not long before their sad demise the Vicinal marked their centenary in 1985 with a comprehensive celebration on the Coast involving operation of representative trams from different eras. All remaining trams bore this special commemorative sign. There will be similar events in 2010 to mark the 125th anniversary.
[John Bromley]

The standard De Lijn livery suits both the seaside character and the trams themselves, but No 6102 seen here at Oostende station sidings in 2005 is unique: it is an eight-axle double-ended car built as a demonstration unit and retained on the Coast mainly for special workings.

This interior view of a Vicinal standard bogie tram gives an impression of the distinctive (and remarkably comfortable) seating.

The unique No 6102 was originally owned by the builders BN and ran in a special livery: it is seen here at Oostende station in July 1982.

Little of the Coast Line now runs on private right of way as distinct from reservation. The approach to Knokke is one example, surviving from the 1890 Brugge – Heist steam tramway. In May 1979 SO motor No 9014 passes the water tower heading for the terminus, with two trailers in tow. The Vicinal renumbered their remaining trams in 1976 and this was formerly 10041, withdrawn three years later. The renumbered cars had a line beneath the initial digit. [John Bromley]

The two ends of the Coast Line have changed over time. In 1964 the north-eastern end ran through Knokke town and terminated at Albertplein in Het Zoute, close to the sea. No 10043 stands on the loop beside the Vicinal station (with a Vicinal bus stop and a red Belgian letter-box nearby). This line would close in 1966. [LRTA, Jack Wyse]

In September 1967 the trams turned round at a new loop near Knokke railway station, on the edge of the town. In this evocative period view a red and cream Vicinal bus waits nearby on the town shuttle service which had replaced the tramway. [Tony Percival]

Apart from paint and new overhead line not much had changed at Knokke by 1984, but the traditional trams had mainly given way to BN-type articulateds. The loop is still in use in 2010 but with an altered passenger shelter.

The south-western end of the line at De Panne was altered in the 1970s when the original seaside loop was replaced by a turning circle around a municipal garden. The small De Panne depot was nearby, now used for museum storage. The photographer's companion rests on the grass after a nightmare two day train journey from Austria to Oostende in August 1984.

The 1986 diversion at Nieuwpoort, which took trams away from the busy main street onto parallel Elisalaan, included a reversing siding at Zonnebloem. In some summer seasons this has been the western terminus of a shuttle service from Oostende, as it was in August 1998.

The Coast Line still passes through part of central Oostende on street and this 1963 view of an SO motor and two differing trailers characterises this section. Motor No 9947 entered service in July 1957 and was withdrawn in 1982.

Marie Joséplein is the main central Oostende stop and was once the terminus of local services. BN No 6010 passes in July 1986. The potentially destructive effect of the now-removed front coupler is all too apparent. [John Bromley]

Viewed from the opposite direction looking towards De Panne Marie Joséplein was still busy in 2005 and is now protected from road traffic. Siemens No 6053 pauses on its way from Westende to Oostende Station. Note the handsome station building on the left, incorporating a ticket office. This is a lonely survivor of several such Vicinal buildings, which included a larger version outside Oostende railway station blown up at the end of the Second World War. This fine example has been restored.

Like most European cities Oostende has changed greatly since the Second World War. Here SO No 9006 is running alongside the inner harbour, with a characteristically varied train composed of an NO trailer and a Destelbergen trailer heading for the turning loop at Westende. The road in the foreground was once a bridge across the inner harbour, removed when part of the dock was filled in. The tower block stands roughly on the site of the old Stad railway station, and the older brick buildings in the far background are those seen in some of the earlier black-and-white views in this book, overlooking the pre-1954 Vicinal station. [John Bromley]

1932-built baggage motor No 10019 is seen in front of Oostende Maritime station in June 1969 whilst shunting. The view also shows the features of the post-war 'Destelbergen' trailers, in this case No 19544: comparison with other illustrations will show that these new-built cars of 1954-5 differed from the standard cars in their flatter roof line and especially their hopper-type side window ventilators in place of the full-drop windows of the older cars. Most lasted until the 1970s. [John Bromley]

The Coast Line was served latterly by three depots, the largest at Oostende which was also equipped for major repairs and construction. The site was that of the original 1885 steam tram depot, greatly enlarged in 1908 to house the new electric fleet. The main running shed is seen here in September 1967, occupied by SO motors and standard trailers. The depot's day-to-day functions have much diminished since the development of the maintenance and storage area near Oostende station. [Tony Percival]

Although the photograph is badly decayed it is included as a rare view of the interim arrangements required at Knokke when the communal council banned tram traffic through the main street. In August 1963 the two 'Destelbergen' trailers at the rear of this train are being drawn back by a baggage-motor, to allow the SO unit to turn using the loop at the back of the depot. It would then back onto the far end of the repositioned trailers. This awkward manoeuvre continued until completion of the new turning circle nearby.

A second large depot is located close to the present Knokke terminus, and apart from storage sheds includes a large loop useful for turning cars when required. In September 1963 the 1930-built shed housed an SO motor, trailers, and a Vicinal bus. The start of the private right-of-way towards Heist is on the right, at this date yet to be equipped with catenary overhead and heavy rail and ballast. There was a third depot at De Panne until 1998. [The late Joseph Jessel Jr]

Maintenance work is unremitting, especially on the difficult and sometimes unstable ground along the Coast. In September 1967 near De Haan a works crew replacing sleepers were using 'narrow' standard No 9994 (built 1932 and housed at Knokke) as their gang car. [Tony Percival]

Standard car 9778 of 1930, transferred from Kortrijk, features in this 1967 view near Oostende Depot: notice the warning stripes around the dash and the 'non-coast' pantograph. The gang are lifting the original double track in the centre of Nieuwpoortsesteenweg, part of the original 1885 steam tramway: it will be replaced by a single line for depot access on the right-hand verge. [Tony Percival]

Some 'narrow' standards worked in passenger service on the Coast, including 9817 (ex-9985 of 1933) transferred from Kortrijk in 1963. It is seen here in 1964 in the entrance to Oostende depot, signed for an Oostende – Bredene shuttle service. There was no loop at Bredene so double-ended trams like this were essential. [LRTA Frank Hunt]

It is hard to recapture now the traditional atmosphere on parts of the Coast. In this 1963 view a tram and trailer make an evening stop at Wenduine Molen. The space on the left is now the westbound carriageway. [The late Joseph Jessel Jr]

Even by the 1960s growing road traffic required better level crossing protection: an SO motor heads a post-war 'Destelbergen' trailer across a deserted highway by the Wenduine windmill. [The late Joseph Jessel Jr]

On the cover and elsewhere in this book we have glimpsed the once-empty dune landscape. By the 1970s the main road had become a dual carriageway and pedestrian crossing signals were needed to reach the tram stop at Bredene-Campings. In August 1979 SO motor No 9024 (renumbered in 1976 from 10050) heads an NO trailer (9452 ex-19700) and standard trailer 9529 (ex-19679 ex-10005). Notice the old track and overhead line equipment. [John Bromley]

Nearby the changes have been even more dramatic. This is Bredene Dunes in July 1986, with the original roadside reservation which ran against the dunes on the left replaced by central reservation and heavy-duty overhead line. No 6032 heads for Oostende. [John Bromley]

Some major changes took place along the Coast in the 1980s. A lengthy diversion was opened along Elisalaan around Nieuwpoort in 1986, taking trams away from the congested sea-side main street.

Towards the north-east end of the route the major dock works at Zeebrugge required new bridges across the entrance locks. This Oostende-bound tram is crossing one of them in July 2008, a view taken from the visiting liner 'QE2'!
[M.R. Taplin]

The 1998 extension back to De Panne railway station at Adinkerke, seen here in July 2005, created a model intermodal terminus: BN No 6030 waits across the platform from a Belgian Railways multiple unit, with the bus stance on the right.

Two views which capture the character of the Coast Line: in September 1963, in a scene typifying an off-season train of the era, SO motor No 10051 with a 'wide standard' trailer and a luggage van at the rear is pictured near De Haan, on rural track with Vicinal catenary masts, a far cry from the clamour of the resort towns. [The late Joseph Jessel Jr]

This scene sums up the Coast perfectly: on the exposed section near Raversijde a boy on a bicycle admires westbound BN motor No 6049 en route for Westende in the summer of 1986. This is the oldest section of electric tramway on the coast. [John Bromley]

Sadly, few early cars from the Coast Lines were preserved, and none of the iconic types. Two that escaped the torch were 'luggage motor' No 10020 of 1932 and its similar antecedent No 9965 of 1911, a rare survivor of the OB. They are both seen here at the Vicinal Museum at Schepdaal, which reopened in 2009 after several years of closure. SO 9014 (p.49) is also preserved.

Nearing Nieuwpoort the tramway passes a solemn place in Belgian history. The great monument on the right commemorates King Albert I of the Belgians (reigned 1909 - 1934) who led his army here in 1914-8 when it was the end of Allied front line and the very point where the sluices were opened in 1914 to flood the land in the distance as a successful defence against German advance. There is a moving British memorial nearby. Westbound BN No 6018 is crossing the IJzer River at what is now a peaceful spot.

Pictures elsewhere have shown Oostende Depot in full use (see page 55). By 2009 the building had been partially rebuilt and the whole complex reduced in size. If current plans materialise it will be replaced by a new depot alongside the tramway north-east of Oostende Station.

We end the colour section with an iconic coastal view, the sea-side tramway at Raversijde. In August 2009 a Siemens car heads east on the seasonal shuttle service from Westende: at the height of the season half the trams operated beyond Oostende to De Haan. The accumulation of wind-blown sand is very clear, a reminder that Blackpool will not be the only place where modern trams co-exist with the sea. In the background the towers of Middelkerke show how the area has been transformed since the first electric trams ran here in 1897.

5.3 Upgrading and renewal

From the mid-1960s development along the Coast had a major impact on the tramway. The Ministry's progressive upgrading of the main coastal road, the Koninklijkebaan ('Royal Road'), into a dual carriageway required relocation of stretches of tracks much onto central reservation, and further encroachment onto the dunes. Examples were at Bredene in 1967-8 and further north-east towards Wenduine in 1969. The growing volume and speed of road traffic, much now unaccustomed to tramways, required extension of light-controls at crossings where road and rail intersected. More catenary overhead was installed.

A different factor led to track relocation in Nieuwpoort (Bad). Increasing traffic congestion led the commune to restrict the main road near the sea to one-way westbound traffic in 1968, with eastbound trams continuing against the flow. This unsatisfactory arrangement continued until 1986 when new tracks were opened in parallel Elisalaan, some distance inland. This improved traffic circulation but of course took the transport artery away from a main commercial area. Further north-east the vast development of the port facilities at Zeebrugge, with a major dock complex inland of the tramway, required new bridges across the broad entrance channel, and after lengthy temporary works, another diversion in 1982 over an alternative inland route enabled trams to continue their journeys whilst vessels locked through the dock entrance. At Oostende the 1954 Vicinal station was replaced by a far larger edifice including staff accommodation. The group of storage sidings nearby was enlarged to act as the principal operating base, lessening use of the awkward route to the depot at Nieuwpoortsesteenweg, retained for repairs and overhaul. Some tram refurbishment has also been carried out in Knokke depot.

Finally each terminus of the tramway was altered. The De Panne – Adinkerke section operated during the summer of 1955 but was then open only intermittently until it closed after the summer season in 1956. The closure of the tracks through Knokke required a new terminal loop at the end of the private right of way near the depot. In De Panne property development displaced the tramway from its single-line loop near the sea, and a smaller turning circle was built around a traffic roundabout at Esplanade in 1977, with a link to the nearby depot. Overall the character of the Coast and its tramway changed substantially by the 1980s, road enlargement being accompanied by replacement of traditional buildings with high-rise blocks at such places as Wenduine. Reminders of the older character do remain, for example at De Haan and on the spectacular sea-front section south-west of Oostende, but much of the route is now urban in character.

The availability of the newer type N cars (see chapter 6) made it possible to provide modern trailer cars for the Coast at last. The converted type-NO trailers neatly matched the SO motors as seen in this view of No 19696 at Oostende in 1967: the train door fitted in conversion at each end is clearly visible as are the brake connections. The destination box was later covered with red glass.

5.4 Preparing for the BN's

The most important innovation was a new fleet of rolling stock, the first complete re-equipment in the line's history. This followed a review of the long-term needs of the Vicinal's two remaining tramway networks, i.e. on the Coast and around Charleroi. The new design emerged as a two-section, six-axle articulated car in two variants, double-ended for Charleroi, single-ended for the Coast (also geared for higher speed). (The cars are described in chapter 6). In preparation for the new fleet there were two essential requirements. The relatively light track, which partly lacked proper ballast, needed replacement with heavier rail of modified profile, and as it had been decided that the coastal version of the BN tram would be single-ended, additional intermediate turning loops were required. These works were largely carried out between 1977 and 1985. Secondly the new cars, especially if working in multiple as intended, had higher power demands than their predecessors (456 kW each compared with about 200 kW for type-SO). This necessitated complete renewal of the overhead line and feeder cables and the reinforcement of power supplies through additional and enlarged sub-stations. This was done between 1977 and 1985. By the mid-1980s the traditional tramway infrastructure had largely disappeared, as the illustrations show. Heavy, well-ballasted rail was in place, and tensioned catenary overhead with heavier support masts had been erected, the latter not always attractive. Stopping places were also improved.

Meanwhile the first BN trams had been delivered, with prototypes arriving by June 1980, some months later than expected.

Tower wagon LW3 is seen here at work at Blankenberge in September 1967. This tram was rebuilt after the war on the frames of 'OB'-type passenger car No 9230, which was largely destroyed by fire in 1944.
[Tony Percival]

This is the 1954 Vicinal station at Oostende with the wholly-renewed overhead installed in 1982 and a new BN-type single-ended tram heading for Knokke. The station would be rebuilt again ten years later.

BN-type No 6035 is passing the sensational Thermae Palace Hotel in Oostende: the new heavy-weight centre poles are only too obvious [John Bromley]

Tests with Oostende prototype No 6000 were carried out between Mariakerke and Middelkerke and from September 1980 it operated some public services. The first double-ended Charleroi car, No 6100, was delivered there in August 1980. At this point the programme began to be modified.

The intention had been that the coastal production series would be built and delivered first, because the existing infrastructure in Charleroi could not accommodate 2.50m-wide rolling stock. But the coastal tests revealed unsatisfactory performance of the prototype bogies and a decision was made to modify and complete the Charleroi series and to assign these temporarily to the Coast. Seven production cars from this fleet were in service during the high summer of 1981, mainly operating two-unit pairs on the Oostende – Knokke section where enhanced power was available. In all 37 of the 54 6100-series trams were delivered temporarily to Oostende, the last at the end of June 1982.

Amongst the Belgian government's intentions in financing light rail development was to enhance opportunities for exports, and efforts were made to interest foreign governments and undertakings in the achievements of Belgian industry. In practice almost the only fruit of this policy was the light rail system in Manila, Republic of the Philippines, party financed by a favourable loan from the Belgian government and designed and equipped by BN, ACEC and their affiliates. The first line of this system, on which work started late in 1981, was opened in 1984-5 and equipped with articulated units originally similar to those supplied to the Vicinal. In preparation for the Manila order, two BN units were tested on Manila-type standard gauge bogies in 1981 and 1982, using the Tervuren line in Brussels. A further promotional venture came to a near-disastrous end in April 1981 when a Coastal demonstration tram carrying the Ambassador of Costa Rica and staff collided violently with another tram near Raversijde, severely injuring several of those on board. No further orders for BN-type cars ever eventuated (and San José never received a light rail line). Parts of the two damaged trams were later incorporated by BN into a new demonstration eight-axle double-ended tram, numbered 6102, which was mainly used for emergency purposes.

The completed production units, Nos 6001 to 6049 with modified bogies, were finally delivered between August 1982 and December 1983, mostly entering service within a few days. Accordingly most of the Charleroi cars left the Coast between September 1982 and October 1983, the main parts of the Charleroi system having opened between 1976 and 1983. The last of the old fleet of motors and trailers was withdrawn from normal service in March 1982, an important finale as some components had been in use at Oostende for over half a century.

5.5 The end of the Vicinal

Another finale followed the federalisation of Belgium in the 1980s, which led directly to the end of the NMVB/SNCV. In response to national legislation in August 1988 two independent regional operating entities were established, the *Vlaamse Vervoer Maatschappij* (VVM) in the Flemish region, and the *Société Régionale Walonne du Transport* (SRWT) in the Walloon region. The former adopted the trading name 'De Lijn' ('the route'), and inherited the Coast Line as well as the city tramways in Antwerpen and Gent. The new administrations began operation on 1 January 1991 and after a year of finalising financial and estate details, the Vicinal was wound up on 1 January 1992 after 106 years.

5.6 Further improvement and extension

Despite extra capacity provided by the centre sections added to all the remaining BN cars by 2003 the continuing rise in traffic again left the system short of vehicles and after trials in 2004 a number of newly-built 'Hermelijn' series Siemens all-low-floor cars, primarily intended for Gent and Antwerpen, has operated on the Coast each summer when requirements in their home cities are reduced. The loaned cars required various modifications, including re-profiled wheels and addition of extension pieces at the doors to compensate for their narrower body width. From 2007 ten of these trams were in a shared pool available to both Gent and the Coast. They have latterly operated on short workings between Oostende and Westende (of course the first coastal section to be electrified).

Suggestions for the re-extension of the Coast Line at its western end, from De Panne to Adinkerke (De Panne railway station), first surfaced in the 1970s and were subject to repeated studies before work began in September 1996. There were several advantages in the project, involving some 3 km of new track partly on a new route and partly following the old roadside alignment through the woods, abandoned in 1956. It opened up a new and convenient cross-platform railway connection at De Panne station, on a National Railways line electrified in 1996.

The route would also serve a popular and long-established theme park ('Meli', now renamed 'Plopsaland'), and would offer extensive purpose-built park-and-ride facilities adjacent to the station and close to an exit from the E40 motorway, facilities difficult to provide closer to the built-up coastal area. Finally a purpose-built tram/bus depot at Adinkerke would replace the unsuitable facilities at De Panne. The new line was opened on 1 July 1998, the first coastal line extension for over sixty years.

6. Rolling stock

6.1 Steam equipment

It is only possible briefly to mention here the vast history of steam-era locomotives and rolling stock (the Vicinal had 838 steam engines and 11,475 other non-electric vehicles in 1925). The system's universal standards ensured that such stock was readily interchangeable between concessions, and the records show that the coastal lines were operated by 45 locomotives and 115 passenger coaches, all but two of the latter two-axled. The engines were built between 1886 and 1920 and were of the distinctive Vicinal pattern, double-ended with 0-6-0 wheel arrangement, enclosed motion and body-sides, and an overall canopy roof. The rapid growth of the electric network meant that most coastal steam engines had been scrapped or transferred by 1936, but five remained in 1951 when the last steam line closed. There had been over 500 assorted goods wagons, of which 220 remained in 1951: about 35

This extraordinary Arabesque confection is the Kursaal (a concert hall and spa) at Oostende in about 1904. The double track in Van Iseghemlaan is the original steam tramway towards Nieuwpoort and an outbound steam tram (on the right) and accumulator car No 3 are passing. Note that they appear to be running on the left. The crowd on the pavement stands outside the tram shelter. [courtesy MUPDOFER]

There are few pictures of steam locomotives at work on the Coast, but No 653 seen at Houffalize is one of a class of four built in 1914 of which another identical example worked at Oostende until scrapped in 1952

were retained after the end of public goods traffic for works purposes. About 15 steam passenger coaches were rebuilt as electric trailers, and others were used on electric lines. Of the 25 steam-era luggage vans 12 were transferred to run with electric stock and the last remained in service until 1966.

6.2 Electric traction: general considerations

Although the total number of electric motors and trailers on the Coast Line at one time never exceeded 255 their history is complex and has been the subject of at least one lengthy book and several extended articles. Here we summarise the equipment and discuss the main themes. We must first note that the gradual and incremental progress of electrification, extending from 1897 to 1934, meant that there was never a cohesive rolling stock strategy to meet the needs of what became a lengthy interurban light railway. Instead the stock designed for the earliest, relatively short, partly seasonal lines formed the basis of the fleet for the ensuing thirty years or so, even if not wholly suitable. Although altered, some of the earliest cars remained in service until the network began to decline in the 1950s. The retention of elderly trams, especially trailers, and their repeated rebuilding and refurbishment, was a prudent approach to running a seasonal tramway with vast disparity between summer and winter loadings, where investment in a wholly new fleet could not be justified.

It is also noteworthy that the Vicinal were relatively late in adopting bogie vehicles, thereby following general practice in Germany rather than the United States, where as early as 1915 well over half of all tramcars were bogie vehicles. Even in Britain, which often tended towards the modest two axle tram, albeit double-decked, the Manx Electric, Rothesay, and Blackpool & Fleetwood, not wholly dissimilar to the first Belgian Coast lines, each had summer and winter bogie rolling stock before 1914.

Although the pioneer TEOL line used trolley poles, the coastal lines later adopted long rotatable bow-collectors until pantographs arrived with the 'Coast Standard' cars. (The only two-axled cars to use pantographs were Nos 9916 – 9). High winds and salt deposits on coastal overhead line required a distinctive design of Siemens pantograph, and as the illustrations show this featured a double contact strip. From 1976 the two-armed 'Stemmann' pantograph was adopted.

The small series of three open-sided cross-bench cars built for the TEOL in 1899 was characteristic of seaside trams in many parts of the world. In July 1952 No 9998 was caught in Nieuwpoortsesteenweg just outside Oostende depot. These cars were all sadly scrapped by 1956, although today they would be popular in tourist service. [LRTA, Jack Wyse]

6.3 Pre-1914 electric motor cars

We have seen that the first two electric lines were built south-west of Oostende in 1897 (TEOL) and north-east in 1905 (OB). Each was equipped with two axle motor trams characteristic of the period. The TEOL fleet included five accumulator cars (later rebuilt as conventional motors) for the Oostende town service, and three open-sided summer cars.

The original OB fleet grew between 1908 and 1911 as electrification was extended eastwards. The total passenger fleet available by 1914 was 59 motors, with seven motor luggage-vans.

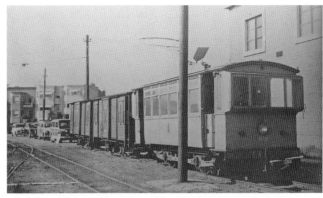

After electrification the Oostende urban lines were largely worked by adapted TEOL cars of 1897 (known as 'phares' from their initial service on the 'lighthouse' route). Their platforms were partly enclosed. Displaced by OB cars after delivery of the Coast Standards some, like 9179, became works cars.

(An attempt has been made in the tables to give a simplified summary of the fleet. The changes and exceptions were so numerous that these are a broad guide only and they are included with reservation. Acknowledgement of sources appears at the end of this chapter, as does an explanation of builders names. It should be noted a comprehensive renumbering meant that numbers appearing on trams after 1976 were different).

Table (i) TEOL motors, (all two-axled, 22 cars)

Fleet Nos	Date	Builders and nick-names	Remarks
1 – 14 (NMVB 9169 – 9182)	1896	Ragheno "Teak" or "Phare"	Known as 'teak' cars from original panelling. Closed bodies with open platforms, seating 24. Rebuilt 1905 with vestibuled windscreens and altered windows. After 1930 used on Oostende and Knokke local services (named 'phare' from use on Vuurtoren branch). Withdrawn 1940 - 55.
15 – 17 (NMVB 9997 – 9999)	1899	Industrie "Courses"	Cross-bench open-sided cars for holiday traffic, seating 26. Remained in service until 1956.
9480 - 9484	1897	Nivelles "Métallurgiques"	Built as accumulator cars prior to overhead electrification, seating 20. Adapted to overhead line and rebuilt twice, in 1909 (to resemble 9212 – 5) and 1948-9 (to the 'Oostende' angular style with three-window bodies), remaining in service until c.1955.

71

Table (ii) OB motors, (all two-axled, 37 cars)

Fleet Nos	Date	Builders and nick-names	Remarks
9212 - 9215	1906 - 1908	Ragheno "Westende"	Closed clerestory cars with vestibuled platforms, seating 24. Six-window bodies, 2.40m wide. Originally gated platforms, later with doors. After 1930 ran on Adinkerke and Veurne etc lines until withdrawn by 1956.
9228 - 9251	1908 - 1909	Ragheno "OB"	Similar to 9212 series. 2 cars destroyed 1914-18, and No 9230 burned out 1944 and rebuilt as tower car LW3. Withdrawn 1952-6.
9470 - 9477	1911	Dyle "OB"	Similar to 9212 series. Withdrawn 1956-8.

These 'OB' cars were the core of the fleet until 1930, and their exceptional 2.55 m width established the broader loading gauge on the coastal lines. From 1930 they worked the newly-electrified branch lines until closure in the 1950s. Although there were detailed variations these trams had a distinctive 'family' style.

A special feature of the coastal lines was the 'motorpakwagen' or 'luggage-motor', in effect a small electric locomotive incorporating van space for luggage and packages. These versatile vehicles, also used for goods, shunting, and works purposes, could haul substantial trains of trailers and were used especially for special workings operating in connection with main line trains, for example for school parties or servicemen. (Three further such vans were added in 1932 and are included here for completeness. These cars were 2.46 m wide with end 'train' doors).

Table (iii) Motor luggage-vans, (two-axled, 10 cars)

Fleet Nos	Date	Builders	Remarks
9950 - 9954	1909	Franco - Belge	Withdrawn 1963 - 67
9965 - 9966	1911	Franco - Belge	Withdrawn 1959 - 61
10019 - 10021	1932	Godarville	Withdrawn 1971 - 73

Oostende depot is still equipped for major repairs. In this post-war view OB-type No 9212 receives attention in the centre, whilst 'Coast Standard' No 10001 on the left is raised on jacks to allow its bogies to be removed. It appears that motor replacement is in progress. On the far right is the body of one of the cross-bench trailers.

Taken in April 1954 this view of 'OB' No 9472 outside Oostende-Stad station shows its final condition, working on the town local service 4 to Slijkens which would be withdrawn, with the tram itself, two years later. This view shows properly the characteristic 'coast' destination sign, a coloured 'plaque' fitted to a bracket on the dash. Roller destination signs did not appear until the first SO motors arrived in 1956. [Tony Percival]

This broadside view of OB motor No 9241 of 1908 shows it in near original condition, with roof-mounted route boards and open-sided platforms with ornate ironwork and gates. The arch-windowed saloons were little altered during the cars' nearly fifty year active life. Notice that the place names are rendered in French.

The attractive 1932 series of luggage-motors were regularly used for shunting duties at Oostende, adding and removing trailers from main-line trains. No 10019 is seen in front of the distinctive Maritime station in 1960 shunting a standard trailer. These cars had end doors for train use and also the illuminated number cubes above the cab (long unused). [John Bromley]

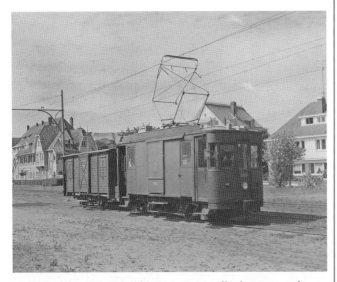

The last of the six original baggage motors (built 1909 – 11) continued in use until 1967, often used for works purposes. No 9953 is seen here in works brown livery on the siding at De Haan, attached to a closed van.

6.4 Additional trams, 1914 - 29

When full operation resumed after the Great War a relatively limited fleet of 57 passenger motors (two cars had been destroyed in the war) was available for the now longer lines extending from Westende to Het Zoute. *SELVOP*, assuming the concession in 1927, faced the large task of commissioning electrification over the remainder of the western route as far as De Panne and Veurne, and of starting through electric service over the whole 70 km between De Panne and Het Zoute, with later additions of the branch services to Adinkerke, Brugge, and Sluis, completed by 1934. Some new trams had been delivered after the war, in some cases long delayed from pre-war orders.

They included the first four bogie motors, but most trams new to the Coast were transferred from other Vicinal undertakings. If there seems to be a slight air of improvisation in the movement of cars in small batches from other parts of the Vicinal system, this flexibility was of course a strength of the national organisation with its common technical standards. The cars involved are listed next.

Table (iv) Motor trams received at Oostende, 1919 – 29 (29 cars, two-axled unless stated)

Fleet Nos	Date	Builders and nick-names	Remarks
9025 - 9029	1901	E&H "Observatoire"	Early open-ended motors built for Brussels service (hence nickname). Flat-roofed 6-window bodies, seating 20. To Oostende in 1928 – 29, withdrawn by 1956.
9050 - 9051	1901	E&H "Observatoire"	Closed cars (series 9048 – 85) built for Brussels. To Oostende from Spa in 1928 – 29, withdrawn by 1932.
9096 - 9111	1897	Nivelles "Liège"	4 cars (9096, 9098, 9102, 9111) from series 9086 – 9113 built for independent Ixelles – Boondael metre-gauge line in Brussels. Six-window saloons seating c.20, later with enclosed platforms. To Oostende from Liège 1928. First cars to be rebuilt in 1932 to "Oostende" angular style with four-window bodies and withdrawn by 1955.
9499 - 9502	1919	B&M "Titanic"	Very large closed bogie cars, seating 48, with clerestory roofs, 12-window bodies. Returned to Brussels by 1929.
9511 - 9514	1918	Roeulx "Roeulx"	Five-window saloons, 2.40m wide seating 24. To Oostende from Antwerpen 1928. Rebuilt to resemble OB cars 9470 – 77 and ran in Oostende local service until 1955.
9573 - 9574	1923	La Hestre "Manage"	To Oostende 1924. 2 class cars. Rebuilt as angular flush-panelled "Oostende" type 1938 – 40 with three-window bodies (see also 9596, 9598). Withdrawn by 1955.
9596 and 9598	1923	Seneffe "Seneffe"	Five-window saloons seating 20, open-sided platforms, from series 9561 – 9598. To Oostende from Leuven 1924. With 9573, 9574 (above) rebuilt with new "Oostende" type three-window bodies 1938-40, and ran in local service until 1955.
9623 - 9628	1920	Energie "Bogota"	Closed 32 seat clerestory bogie cars of 'Bogota' type built for export but not sent. 5-window 2 class bodies, archaic appearance. 6 cars of series to Oostende from Brussels in 1929. Partly remodelled 1929 with larger platforms and flat ends, added doors. Rebuilt as trailers 19450 – 5 in 1948. 9628 ran experimentally in three-axle form until c. 1948.

Thus 29 passenger motors were added to the fleet by 1929, although not all remained in Oostende, bringing the total to 86.

Although they belong to a later period it is appropriate to mention here the last examples of entirely new two-axle trams to enter service in Oostende, albeit briefly. In 1932 *SELVOP* sought to enhance its aging fleet of smaller trams and procured four modern cars, a sub-fleet of a large group of about 140 similar cars known as the 'Braine-le-Comte' series, but differing from the others in their 2.40 m 'coastal' width and end doors.

At 10.45 m overall in length, they were significantly larger than the earlier cars (the 'OB' type were 8.9 m long). The four smart trams arrived new in Oostende in 1932 but oddly remained for only a few months, being returned to Charleroi in 1933. Allegedly they were too slow for coastal operation and there may have been other problems. They were the last wholly-new two axle cars to run on the Coast.

(Table v) Cars 9916 – 9 (4 cars)

Fleet Nos	Date	Builder	Remarks
9916 - 9919	1932	Ragheno	Wide wooden flush-sided two-axled cars with six-window bodies seating 32, closed platforms, and tapered ends. Centre-mounted pantographs. Left Oostende 1933

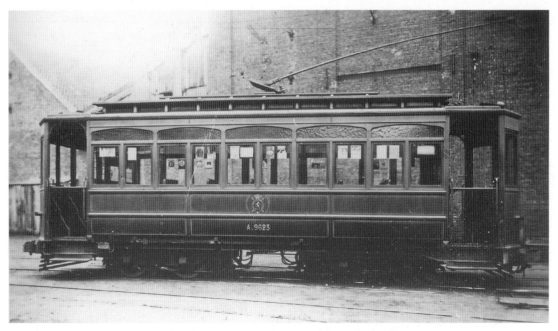

Bogie trams were rare on the coast before 1930, but six cars of a series originally built in 1920 for export were assigned to Oostende in 1929. Named 'Bogotas' from their intended destination they were of massive but archaic appearance for the era. No 9623, one of the cars which eventually came to the coast, is seen here in original condition with a trolley pole and Vicinal green livery.

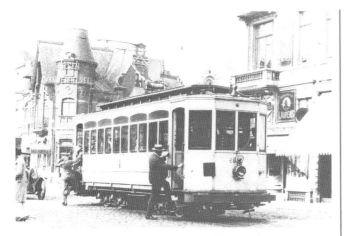

Another car in the 'Bogota' series is seen here in operation about 1930 at Petit Paris, Oostende, fitted with a bow collector and in 'Empain' yellow livery: these trams, later rebuilt with extended platforms, generally operated on town services. The strange structure on the extreme left of the picture was an elevated police box from which the town's first traffic lights were controlled.

It is hard to believe that car No 9480 nominally began life in 1897 as one of the accumulator cars and was twice rebuilt. This was its post-1948 style when very little of the original vehicle can have survived as it had a new body and a second-hand truck. This later three-window form of body was attractive but the tram lasted less than ten years before withdrawal. It was photographed on the Kaai at Oostende with the Stad station tower in the distance, by then lacking its clock.

One of the 1932 'Braine-le-Comte' cars (Nos 9916 – 9) is seen in Oostende depot yard during its brief stay on the Coast. These smart little trams were specially designed for coastal service, with wide bodies and train doors, but failed to satisfy and were shipped back to Charleroi within months. They were the only modern four-wheelers to run on the system. [Courtesy MUPDOFER]

We shall look next at the spectacular change brought by the new 'Standard' trams, and then summarise the substantial fleet of trailers.

6.5 The bogie revolution

In anticipation of the completion of electrification the full length of the Coast in 1929 SELVOP reviewed its rolling stock requirements and in particular sought faster and more comfortable cars suitable for long journeys. The Vicinal now had experience with bogie cars following the introduction of the 'Bogota' and 'Titanic' types in 1919-20, but SELVOP's thoughts seem initially to have turned to three-axle or radial-axle cars, a cheaper expedient. After experiments conducted using 1897 car 9484 this concept was discarded, and the outcome of continuing discussions between the Vicinal and SELVOP was an entirely new series of large bogie motors which became the first of the so-called 'standard' type.

It is interesting that the coastal management chose not to specify multiple-unit equipment, which would have increased operational flexibility. The technology was available – m.u. trams were entering service in Berlin from 1929 and there had been trials on the Vicinal– and the characteristics of the route and its traffic would seem to favour it. But the economic austerity following the 1929 Crash perhaps discouraged elaborate ventures, and it was not until the BN cars that short-lived m.u. operation came to the line.

6.6 The 'Coast Standard' cars (35 cars, series 9729 - 10054)

The new trams introduced on the Coast from 1930 began a new chapter in Vicinal rolling stock history. The network's 'standard' bogie motor trams would be built and rebuilt over a period of nearly thirty years and totalling exactly 400 units represented a sizeable modern fleet, although still fewer than half the total number of electric cars in the national fleet. Of these the distinctive batch of 35 'Coast Standards', originally numbered in the series 9729 to 10054, were built in 1930 (7), 1932 (14) and 1933 (14, these having been converted from trailer cars built new in 1930-2). They were designed for the particular circumstances of the Coast operation: wider than normal, taking advantage of the Coast's wide track-spacing (2.40 m against the standard 2.20 m); powerful, capable of hauling the multiple trailers needed to handle Coast summer traffic; with end (or 'train') doors to enable a conductor ('ontvanger' or 'receveur', *never* 'conducteur' – French for 'driver' !) to move from car to car

This view of the sidings near Oostende station shows a gathering of miscellaneous rolling stock typical of the 1950s with two of the remaining 1930-built 'Coast Standard' motors, including No 10042 in the centre. The cars were little changed from their original state and still look majestic. There is a two-axled trailer on the extreme left. By the summer of 1956 many Standards had been withdrawn to provide frames and bogies for construction of 'SO' motors, and 10042 would be one of the last conversions, in June 1957. Its body later formed the basis of 'new' bogie trailer No 19680.

for fare collection; and divided into two compartments offering first and second class seats, a feature of the route until after the Second World War. The cars were double-ended with wooden bodies, attractively styled, with four 47-kW motors (initially), and 'Pennsylvania'-type cast steel bogies. They took advantage of modern motor design and had smaller-diameter wheels and hence lower floors than earlier trams. They were originally painted a deep cream colour (so-called 'Empain Yellow'), with silver roofs and blue lining. Unusually for the Vicinal these standards never had end indicator boards or 'plaques', but carried a coloured service number plate on the dash and long route boards beneath the side windows. They were originally fitted with Berlin-like roof-mounted illuminated display cubes for service numbers, but these proved to be impracticable and were speedily taken out of use although they remained in position. Some cars were initially equipped with bow collectors, and their prominent domed roofs distinguish them from later standard cars.

The Coast Standards, together with the somewhat heterogeneous fleet of trailers, now met most of the needs of the main-line service, and its extension to Brugge. They served in one form or another for up to fifty years, and it is notable that their strong wooden bodies resisted both exceptionally heavy loading and the destructive effects of salt-laden wind, perhaps better than contemporary metal cars would have done. The older two-axle cars survived on branch line and urban services until these were withdrawn in the 1950s.

Table (vi) Coast Standards

Fleet Nos	Date	Builders	Remarks
Series 9729 – 10054 (35 cars)	1930 - 1933	Familleureux	Wide wooden cars on steel frames and Pennsylvania bogies, originally seating 16 first, 24 second class with provision for 88 standing. 13.46 m long (44 feet, long by UK standards, comparable to Grimsby & Immingham 'long' GCR cars).

A few 'narrow' standards made their way to the Coast. No 9817 (formerly 9985), seen in front of the Maritime station in August 1964 on a shuttle service, was built in 1933 and rebuilt later following a fire. It was transferred from Kortrijk in 1963. Comparison with earlier illustrations shows how the car differed from the Coast Standards: different roof profile and end windows, and a prominent destination sign. It was fitted in Oostende with a 'coast type' heavy pantograph and Westinghouse air brakes.

6.7 Other standards

The superiority of the Coast Standards was obvious, and a total of 117 similar wooden-bodied cars was built by 1933 for use across most of the national Vicinal network, although of narrower body width. These were followed by 248 cars with steel bodies before production ceased in 1947. Before 1940 some of these 'narrow' standard cars were loaned to the Coast from other groups during the high season, and later others were permanently transferred, as withdrawal of the traditional two-axled cars and the introduction of the single-ended SO motors left the undertaking with few trams to deal with extra runs where no turning circles existed, such as for the Oostende race traffic. Two of the original standards were retained for a time, and narrow standards 9729 (formerly 9984) and 9817 (formerly 9985) were transferred from Kortrijk in 1963: both had been allotted spare numbers in the 'Coast' series. They were modified in Oostende by the addition of Westinghouse brakes. Similar cars Nos 9778 and 9994 followed in 1966, and were used as works cars.

6.8 Type SO (28 cars, series 9818 - 10054)

The Coast finally saw the last fine flowering of the Vicinal standard tram. The original wooden bogie cars were stylistically obsolescent by the 1950s, but their heavy steel frames, bogies, and equipment were still serviceable. Although, as will shortly be mentioned, an entirely new fleet had been designed and built for the Vicinal's urban operations, the availability of existing equipment, and the need for economy as the undertaking's financial position worsened, led the Vicinal to resort after 1954 mainly to re-bodying rather than wholly new construction. The final large fleet of Vicinal cars, the 200 'S'-type, wedded the attractive modern body design of the N-type (described later) to existing frames and equipment. For the Coast a special sub-series was built, designated 'SO' for 'S-Oostende', built on the frames of all but four of the surviving Coast Standards but not maintaining their broader body size. Exceptionally they were single-ended, had fixed forward-facing, green-upholstered two-and-one seats with armrests, and were fitted with roller-blind indicators. As was

No 9778 (built 1930) was another 'narrow standard' which came to the Coast in 1966 for use on works duties in place of the withdrawn luggage-motors. In this interesting view taken in September 1967 it is seen in Nieuwpoortsesteenweg with Oostende depot in the far background: the tall building is the Vicinal's local administrative office block, built in 1931-2. The track gang are lifting the double track in the main road, formerly used by local electric services and the steam trams from Nieuwpoort. It would be replaced by a new single depot access track on the right hand edge of the road, reducing conflict with road traffic. This line was, of course, part of the original 1885 Vicinal line, the first on the Coast. [Tony Percival]

Table (vi) Type SO

Fleet Nos	Date	Builders	Remarks
Series 9818 – 10054 (28 cars)	1956 - 1957	Rue Eloy	N-type rounded single-ended metal bodies mounted on former 'standard' frames and roller-bearing bogies, 2.32 m wide, seating 42 mainly on fixed seats, with provision for 58 standing. Train doors at rear.

appropriate to the tourist nature of the line, passenger notices were in four languages. The first test run, with No 10003, was on 16 March 1956.

In addition to the single-ended 'SO' cars, 14 double-ended 'S' and 'SE' type motors came to the Coast between 1966 and 1978 from previous use in Brussels and Antwerpen, and proved useful both to haul trailers and to reverse en route when required. Four were semi-permanently coupled into back-to-back pairs forming useful high-capacity reversible units capable of high speed on special workings

6.9 Trailers

The holiday traffic on the long line could only be handled with such a modest fleet of motor trams by the extensive use of trailers, of which a large and varied fleet was built up, always exceeding the motors in number. Again, down to 1930 these were two-axled cars of relatively unsophisticated design, so that the characteristic train well into the 1950s consisted of a hard-working motor tram with three or more varied trailers. Until the 1920s the Vicinal was almost wholly a 'two-axled' tramway, and the Coast Line typified this. Apart from a mere two ex-steam bogie trailers (Nos 1800 and 1801) impressively rebuilt, the

When new the SO motors worked with older trailers and few trains were homogenous in appearance. The rear trailer in this April 1957 view of a westbound train nearing Oostende is an ex-steam two-axled car. The train is crossing a standard gauge dockyard siding in Slijkensesteenweg, the branch to Slijkens and Bredene Dorp diverging to the right here. The signal on the left-hand traction pole controlled access to the nearby canal bridge.

By August 1957 all 28 'SO' motors were in service, and No 10053 is seen en route to De Panne crossing the elaborate railway bridge outside Oostende Maritime station, with wide standard trailer 19675 in tow. The SOs were not delivered in numerical order: 10003 was the first, 10053 the seventeenth.

Twenty open-sided trailers were built in 1897 matching the cross-bench motors, and were retained for heavy traffic to and from Oostende race-course. An 'OB' motor hauls three of them alongside the Grand Stand in August 1956, their final season before scrapping. [National Tramway Museum, M.J. O'Connor]

This view of trailer No 11589 at Oostende in 1955 typifies the large fleet of two-axled, balconied trailers with distinctive sun visors over the platforms which served the coast for over forty years. They were much modified and varied in number of windows and in roof style. This car, built in 1909, had seven arched windows and a clerestory roof.

This splendid view at Westende is full of the atmosphere of the seaside 1930s, with summer dresses, sun hats, and short-sleeves, somewhat more formal than the fashions of 2010. The fine station building stood between the tracks until demolished to permit road widening. The uniformed 'receveur' stands by the centre trailer ready to blow his whistle. The rearmost trailer (No 8960) is unusual: it is one of four open-sided bogie trailers built in 1923 and allegedly intended for export to Oran, slightly resembling similar cars on the Manx Electric Railway. These cars were rebuilt as closed 'standard'-type trailers in 1942.

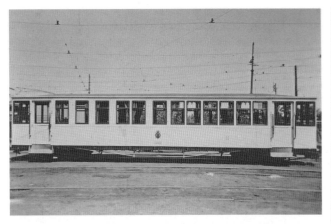

Trailers 1800 and 1801 were further rare examples of bogie trailers. They were built for steam haulage and rebuilt twice, in this form in 1932 which included luxurious first-class accommodation as well as a more utilitarian second-class saloon. They were again rebuilt with a more rounded roof in 1946-7.

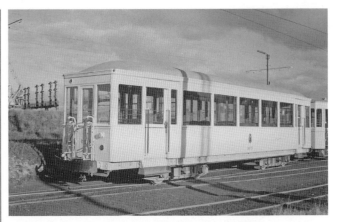

The post-war re-equipment of the Coast line included an influx of bogie trailers, some built new but many converted from older motors. No 19673 is seen in the sidings near Oostende Vicinal station, with the semaphore signals outside the main line Maritime station in the background. This wide car was one of a batch of 32 rebuilt at Oostende depot in 1956 – 7 from older standard motors, in this case No 9942. It remained in service until 1981.

The four-wheeled luggage van was characteristic of the Coast Line until the 1960s, twelve of this type having been built between 1885 and 1904 for steam haulage and adapted for use with electric traction. No 2371 is seen attached to a westbound motor in the new Oostende station in 1957. The 'next tram' clock indicators in the background were a feature of the station. [Tony Percival]

first series of bogie trailers didn't arrive until 1923. Contemporary with the 'Coast Standard' motors a series of matching bogie trailers also arrived, but these were almost immediately withdrawn for conversion to motors. Only much later were new and rebuilt trailers received, and newer surplus cars were cascaded from lines closing elsewhere in Belgium. All these post 1930 bogie trailers had a strong generic similarity but differed in detail, for example in roof profile and in window layout.

Like the first two-axle motors the initial substantial fleet of trailer cars, which totalled 115 by 1928, was basic in design and noted for their noise and relatively hard riding, but a journey on them on a sunny day was part of the holiday experience in less sophisticated times and they are still remembered today as part of a Belgian childhood.

Their history is far too complex to detail here, but the pictures give an impression of their latter-day appearance.

Table (vii) Electric traction trailers before 1930 (all two-axled except where stated)

Fleet Nos	Date	Builders	Remarks
8748 - 8759	1897	Nivelles	Ex TEOL. Open-sided cross-bench cars for summer use, seating 20 - 23. Some retained for race traffic until 1956.
8760 - 8767	1897	Industrie	As above, minor differences. Seating 26. Withdrawn by 1956.
8768 - 8771	1906	Ragheno	First of a series of OB balconied trailers seating 32, some originally semi-open but rebuilt on several occasions with many variations
8867 - 8882	1911	Franco-Belge	As above
8883 - 8892	1911	HSP	As above
8900 - 8901	1919	Franco-Belge	Similar to above, from series 8897 - 8904. In Oostende from 1919 but then transferred to Antwerpen with remainder of series.
8958 - 60; 8963	1923	Nivelles	Four open-sided cross-bench bogie cars type 'Oran', seating 42. Rebuilt as 'standard Destelbergen' trailers 1942.
11564 - 11573	1909	Energie	Built with drop-windows which could originally be lowered completely creating semi-open summer cars, and with distinctive curved sun visors over balconies. Withdrawn by 1955
11574 - 11593	1909	Hiard	As above

The fleet of two-axled closed trailers was repeatedly modified with many variations, but they had a definite generic style which typified the coastal operation until their replacement by cascaded standard trailers and the de-motored N-types in the 1950s and 1960s.

In addition to the above cars specifically built for electric operation, steam-hauled coaching stock also ran on the electric sections and a number of such cars were rebuilt specifically for electric haulage. About forty steam trailers were used, not all rebuilt although exceptions included two long and striking bogie cars (1800 – 1) which were twice rebuilt and remained in stock until 1963. 12 former steam two-axled trailers in the number series 10656 – 11714 were also rebuilt in 1928 with lengthened bodies (type "rallongée").

A well-remembered feature of the coastal lines was the luggage-van or 'pakwagen', delightful balcony-ended two-axle cars equivalent to a British railway guard's van. They had sliding side doors and were designed to handle registered luggage, parcels, and postal traffic, all of which continued into modern times. They were often to be seen either coupled alone to a motor or in a train of trailers. 12 were built between 1885 and 1904, and the last remained in service until 1966.

111 trailers were in use by 1927, of very mixed ancestry. The new bogie trailers delivered in 1930-2 were rebuilt almost immediately and it was 1948 before systematic replacement of the two-axled cars by bogies began, mainly through rebuilding and reconstruction of existing motor trams, but with a few new-builds.

6.10 Type 'NO' trailers
(21 cars, series 19693 – 19713)

The 'N' or 'NO' trailers deserve a section to themselves. The 'N-type' urban trams did not initially concern the Coast, but at the end of their lives came to play an important part in operations and for completeness they will be described here. The Vicinal had planned before 1940 a new series of bogie cars for

The first type-N conversion (into an 'NO' trailer) was No 19693, completed as a trial in 1966. It is seen here at De Haan on 8 June 1966 with the special bogies designed for the class visible: as the N-type motors had body-mounted motors their trucks were unusual. On the SO-motor ahead there can just be seen the huge, traditional oil tail lamp.

Table (ix) Trailers received after 1930 (all bogie)

Fleet Nos	Date	Builders	Remarks
19116 - 19117	1930	Familleureux	Wide-bodied standards. Converted into motors in 1932.
19205 - 19216	1932	Familleureux	As above.
19450 - 19455	1948	Oostende	Rebuilt from 1920 'Bogota' motors 9623 - 8. Withdrawn c. 1955.
19533- 9; 19541 - 8	1952 - 53	Destelbergen	Built new as standard trailers, mainly from spare components. Most in service in 1976.
19549; 19653 - 5	1955 - 58	Rue Eloy	Converted from narrow-bodied standard motors. Withdrawn c. 1966.
19656 – 87	1956 - 57	Oostende	Wide-bodied. Rebuilt from standard motor-car bodies (14 of which had previously been trailers). Most withdrawn 1966 – 8.
19688 – 92	1958	Oostende	Narrow bodied. Rebuilt from standard motors, three of which had previously been motors. Some in service to c.1980.
19693 – 19713	1965 - 68	Rue Eloy	Narrow bodied. Rebuilt from post-war N-type motors (see text).

its city services, and ten prototype vehicles were built between 1941 and 1949, the last four of which introduced an attractive body design, with gracefully curved ends and smooth sides with flush windows. These style features, and a novel cardan-shaft drive system, were incorporated into a fleet of 81 new trams built mainly between 1949 and 1954 and designated 'type 'N' (after the service on which they were first used in Brussels). Abandonment of the services for which they were built sadly condemned them to early withdrawal.

These trams were not designed to haul trailers and accordingly were of little interest to the coastal management, and although two (9272 and 9273) were sent to Knokke after the Brussels metre-gauge system closed in 1978, they never entered service. However the type's bodies and bogies were relatively new, and 21 of the redundant N-types were de-motored and adapted for trailer operation on the Coast in 1965-8, being fitted with end doors. Coupled to the 'SO' motors they formed pleasantly homogenous train sets, and the final cars lasted until replacement by 'BN' articulated cars in 1982.

This gives a total of 83 bogie trailers brought in use between 1948 and 1968.

6.11 The BN series (52 cars)

In 1975 the Vicinal began exploring options for fleet replacement in both Oostende and Charleroi, favouring multiple-unit articulated vehicles which would replace all existing stock and would cope with peak demand with a smaller fleet and fewer staff. It was

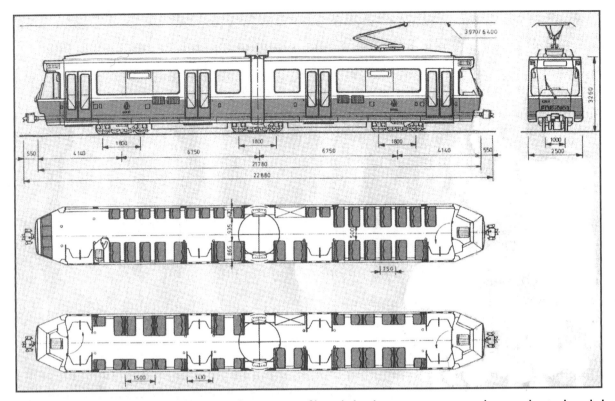

This diagram of the BN types shows the original attractive profile and also the two variant interior layouts: the single-ended 'Oostende' version (above) and the double-ended 'Charleroi' version (below). Both worked in Oostende to begin with.

decided that 50 vehicles would be sufficient for the Coast (the existing fleet of motors and trailers then totalled about 85). The new cars' higher speed and flexibility would bring important economies and efficiencies. After the display of models in 1975 two prototypes were ordered in May 1977, differently configured for the two systems, and the two production fleets were ordered in December 1978, 49 further cars for the Coast and 54 for Charleroi.
These became the 'BN' series (named after their manufacturers in Brugge) which, much modified, continues to handle most of the coastal traffic.

The new cars were six-axle, single-ended articulated vehicles with distinctive tinted windows, and handsome tapered ends facilitating an enclosed driver's compartment with a window for fare collection. The coastal version had fixed forward-facing seats, two-and-two in the front module and two-and-one in the rear.

Retractable steps were fitted. It was originally intended to retain two-person crews and provision was made for a conductor's desk at the rear but this was discarded before operation began.

A schedule speed of between 29 and 39 km/h was planned depending on stop spacing (in practice the coastal tramway offers a schedule speed of about 33 km/h, reputed to be the highest in Europe for a conventional tramway).

Increasing traffic and the requirement for level access for the mobility-impaired led to the addition of centre sections in two phases: the two batches differed, the second having a longer low-floor section with more seats. In appearance the centre sections are not entirely happy having a different profile from the main modules.

The decision to remove the automatic couplers and to end multiple operation may seem surprising given accepted practice elsewhere, but experience showed that the protruding equipment was highly vulnerable and destructive in accidents and that the prevalent salt- and sand-laden air led to unreliability.

A more frequent service of eight-axle cars was believed to be both more robust and more commercially attractive, as has proved to be the case.

Table (x) Type BN (52 cars)

Fleet Nos	Date	Builders	Remarks
6000 - 6049	1980 - 83	BN	Built as six-axle metal-bodied single-ended cars, originally seating 59 with provision for up to 132 standing in crush conditions. Overall length 21.8 metres and width 2.5 metres, i.e. wider than previous 2.4 metre standard. Fitted with monomotor bogies, and chopper control through foot pedals as on BN's PCC-based models. Air, dynamic, and magnetic brakes. Maximum speed 75 km/h. Originally fitted with automatic couplers, mainly removed after 1990. A fourth bogie and low-floor centre section was added to the whole operating fleet in 1993-6 (16 cars, 3.0 m low floor section) and 2002-3 (32 cars, 4.8 metre low floor). These added between 14 and 20 extra seats. Two cars have been scrapped after accidents.
6102	1982	BN	Eight-axle double-ended car built by BN from portions of two cars (6102 and 6103) accidentally damaged on 7 April 1981, also using central module of prototype 6000. Mainly used for breakdown and special purposes.
6131	1982	BN	'Charleroi'-type double-ended car retained on the Coast but taken out of service in 1992 and later scrapped.

Acknowledgements for data in fleet lists to Davies (1984); Block (1991); TTO (1996); and Koenot et al (2006) (see bibliography).

The changes to the BN-types have not improved their appearance. This view shows the difference, with the un-rebuilt rear of 6012 on the right and the remodelled front of 6013 on the left.

Appendix 1

Numbers of cars in the coastal fleet at representative dates

Year	Motors	Trailers
1918	63	94
1928	84	115
1938	108	147
1948	103	152
1958	39	57
1968	38	51
1978	42	46
1988	51	0

Acknowledgement to TTO *Elektrische Trams (1996)* (see bibliography)

Appendix 2
Key to rolling stock builders

B&M:	SA des Usines Baume & Marpent, Morlanwelz and Haine-St-Pierre
BN:	Descendent of *La Brugeoise et Nivelles* (later BN *Spoorwegmaterieel en Metaalconstructies*, Brugge. Now part of Bombardier group.
Destelbergen:	NMVB Gent workshops
D&B:	Dyle et Baclan
E&H:	SA Electricité et Hydraulique, Charleroi (later ACEC)
Energie:	SA d'Energie, Marcinelle
Familleureux:	SA des Ateliers de Construction de Familleureux, Charleroi
Franco-Belge:	Société Franco-Belge, La Croyère
Godarville:	Ateliers de Godarville, Hainaut
Hiard:	Société Hiard & Cie, Haine-St-Pierre (amalgamated with HSP, below)
HSP:	Cie Centrale de Construction, Haine-St-Pierre, La Louvière
Industrie:	SA l'Industrie, Leuven
La Hestre:	Les Forges & Usines de la Hestre, Haine-St-Pierre
Nivelles:	SA Metallurgiques, Ateliers de Nivelles (see BN above, merged 1956)
Oostende:	NMVB workshops, Nieuwpoortsesteenweg, Oostende
Ragheno:	Usines Ragheno, Mechelen
Roeulx:	Les Ateliers du Roeulx SA, Hainaut
Rue Eloy:	NMVB/SNCV Cureghem workshops, Brussels
Seneffe:	Les Forges & Ateliers de Seneffe, Hainaut

7. Present and future
Goed kijken! Ik kan niet wijken!

7.1 De Lijn's achievement

Greater resources, especially with the active support of the now-devolved regional government; cohesive and active management; and above all the growing demand for high-quality public transport common across Western Europe since the 1990s: all these have refreshed and strengthened the coastal tramway in a way hard to foresee thirty years ago. Intermodal links such as that newly built at Adinkerke, a simpler tariff and ticketing system, and good information resources have added to the attractiveness of the tramway. The introduction of free travel for Belgian senior citizens increased seasonal traffic, and more frequent services for a longer period of the year produced higher passenger numbers year on year.

Traffic during July and August grew by over fifty per cent between 1998 and 2002, with 3.2 million rides in those months in 2002. Total ridership has continued to grow, with the two most recent years recording record numbers of journeys:

2007: 12,034,817
2008: 12,134,295

The problems of traffic congestion, especially at the western end of the system, persist. This is the Nieuwpoortlaan in De Panne on an August afternoon in 1998.

Blankenberge was one of the earliest holiday resorts on the Coast and retains some of its gracious buildings. In July 2008 BN No 6004 heads west, with its differently-profiled low-floor centre section apparent. [M.R. Taplin]

The 1998 extension from De Panne to Adinkerke was the first for over sixty years. BN No 6020 stands under the generous roof in August 1998. The train platform is just to the left.

Recalling that in former times the end-to-end service was sometimes reduced to an hourly through car with extras, recent timetables are remarkable. In July and August 2009 94 services left Knokke between 05.31 and 00.31, the high-season throughout journey taking 143 minutes (129 minutes in winter). During most of the day (07.51 to 18.51) six cars an hour ran the whole length of the line. The peak base service requires about 40 BN cars daily out of 48, and as we have seen, low-floor trams are also borrowed from Gent and Antwerpen for supplementary service (some now remain on the Coast). Frequent extras ran between Westende and Oostende in the high season, extended to De Haan in the busiest weeks.

An innovation from November 2007 was a year-round limited stop service between Nieuwpoort and Oostende each weekday, connecting with early-morning inter-city trains. The long-standing summer practice of offering pre-payment from booths ('Lijnwinkels', or 'route shops') lessens delays. About half the 68 intermediate stops are staffed in season. The service is worked from three running depots: the operating base near Oostende station, the elderly depot at Knokke, and the modern bus and tram facility at Adinkerke. Maintenance and some storage is still undertaken at the old Oostende depot, now planned for replacement. The former De Panne depot houses museum cars.

The BN fleet has been progressively refurbished since the mid 2000s, with improved interior fittings, digital destination signs, and visual annunciators in the saloons. De Lijn also has a long-term track maintenance and renewal programme, involving extensive work each winter mainly with single-line working. Some relocation has continued to produce more favourable operating conditions for the tramway, for example through Middelkerke in 2000. Tram priority at certain road crossings was developed from 2008 with detection of approaching trams regulating lights in their favour.

A regrettable series of accidents, arising partly from unfamiliarity amongst visitors, has led to improved foot crossing signage and signals, and a publicity campaign with the catchy slogan *'Goed kijken! Ik kan niet wijken!'* ('Look out! I can't dodge you!').

7.2 Future prospects

De Lijn have announced a series of long-term aspirations for development of public transport across the Province of West Flanders, in a blueprint entitled 'Plan Neptunus'. This covers the period 2007 – 22, and would cost around EUR 430 million to complete.

The coastal tramway is at the heart of the project, and amongst other proposals are the improvement of right-of-way and stops, and improved frequency and speed (the BN rolling stock will require replacement by about 2021). There are also several plans for light rail construction, many involving 'tram-train' use of National Railways tracks, and hence ruling out metre-gauge operation. Proposals examined in detail early in 2008 included the following:

- Koksijde – Veurne;
- De Panne or Veurne to Dunkerque;
- Zeebrugge – Brugge (later possibly to Torhout);
- Oostende – Brugge.

The first project listed, on metre gauge and involving restoration of a route abandoned

This book began with a steamship on the Quay at Oostende. In 2005 a Siemens tram is leaving the turning loop at Oostende station with a car ferry of Trans-Europe Ferries, successors to Belgian Marine, in the background.

under wartime conditions in 1941, reached the stage of detailed studies late in 2008 and an environmental impact study was commissioned in April 2009. The 6.5 km line would involve significant engineering work including a new canal bridge and a tunnel beneath the Koksijde airfield runway.

An intermodal terminal would be built at Veurne, improving long-distance links. A De Panne - Dunkerque link, considered twice before as we have seen, might use the existing standard-gauge rail route, now disused west of the factory at Leffrinckouke, or a parallel route with better traffic potential. This project is also under consideration by the French authorities

In 2008 plans were also announced for comprehensive redevelopment of the Oostende station area, providing much-improved National Railways facilities (although the iconic 1913 main station building will be retained), with an adjoining intermodal terminal incorporating both bus and tram stations and a new tramway turning circle replacing the awkward back-street loop dating from 1954-5.

A new tram depot is planned north-east of the station at Slijkensesteenweg, replacing existing facilities and much improving conditions. A planning application was submitted in June 2009, and the project could be completed by 2014.

The Coast in 2009

De Lijn's success with the Coast line owes much to improved intermodal links. In August 2009 a tram at Adinkerke terminus is flanked by a full range of modes: proper bicycle storage in the foreground, a Belgian Railways' train on the left, the park-and-ride site in the far distance, and a French bus on the right, on the regular service to Dunkerque which might eventually become a tram.

Much has been done in recent years to improve stopping places on the coastal tramway. At Nieuwpoort Stad in the summer of 2009 the tram stop is part of an attractive renewal project, with a new 'lijnwinkel' or ticket office and improved platforms and seating.

The village of Lombardsijde between Westende and Nieuwpoort is one of few places on today's coastal tramway with echoes of the traditional Vicinal. The tramway still hugs the kerb in the main street, but the massive modern overhead line supports give the game away. This was part of the original 1885 steam tramway.

Although most rolling stock on the coast has been single-ended since the 1950s, the borrowed Siemens cars include some double-ended versions shared with Gent. This is Westende loop in August 2009 on the last day of the seasonal shuttle service: Siemens No 6333 is one of the 'Coast/Gent' pool of 2007 (number series 6332 - 6335) with doors on both sides, as can be seen. 2.3 m wide and 29.6 m long these cars seat 58. The similar Antwerpen versions are single-ended (for example No 6051 on p. 42) and seat 74.

The centre sections added to BN cars since 1993 facilitate level access, and more recently platforms have been re-profiled to match them. In the background note the retractable step fitted to the original modules.

'Tram Priority': prominent warning signs are now provided the length of the tramway.

The major depots on the undertaking are at Oostende and Knokke but there was also a small depot at De Panne now replaced by a bus/tram installation at Adinkerke. The neat building is used for storage of heritage trams.

Access to the original Oostende depot is by a narrow side street and a back gate, where 6022 is pausing in August 2009. The digital destination sign is able to display a warning message for following road traffic.

We have seen (page 37) that the SO motors were delivered to the Coast using the Vicinal's heavy transporter. An even longer modern equivalent is used to convey the Siemens cars from and back to Antwerpen or Gent for seasonal service. The deck is fitted with both standard- and metre-gauge tracks. The equipage was waiting at Oostende depot on 31 August 2009 at the end of the summer timetable. In the background are De Lijn's area offices, which replaced the 1930s building seen on page 57.

8. Acknowledgements and bibliography

8.1 Acknowledgements

Thanks are first due to Colin Skelsey who was on that first Vicinal tram ride in 1959, to visit the sadly-vanished site of the British naval raid on Zeebrugge Mole on St-George's Day 1918. Ron Gee encouraged us to take up again a project first planned in 1997 but put aside during work on our recent Brussels book, and also suggested the main title. Many friends have been helpful on visits to Belgium or in supplying and correcting illustrations and information, notably the late Jack Wyse, Richard Buckley, Tim Figures, John Haggar, Roger Jones, and Granville King. Warm thanks to our Production Editor, Sue Graves.

Eric Smith corrected many factual and linguistic infelicities, and kindly supplied timetable details. The text was also expertly read in draft by Ron Gee who made many important suggestions. The remaining errors are entirely the authors'. This book has drawn mainly on published information and is not an official publication of De Lijn. The opinions expressed are solely those of the authors.

Steve Xerri again kindly advised on processing maps and illustrations. The book was originated on a Macintosh iMac model 8.1 2.4 GHz PowerPC, using HP Scanning and Adobe Photoshop CS3 processing software.

Unless otherwise stated illustrations are by the authors or from their collections, but a number of generous individuals kindly made their pictures available. Our thanks to Mike Beamish, the late Joseph Jessel Jr, Mike Taplin, and especially John Bromley and Tony Percival who generously provided a treasure-trove of photographs dating from 1954 onwards. Special thanks are also due to M. Jean Schleich of the Belgian documentation centre *MUPDOFER* for access to rare pictures (see www.mupdofer.be for details of this superb organization).

Photographs from the collections of Jack Wyse, Frank Hunt, and Peter Atkinson are reproduced by courtesy of the Light Rail Transit Association, London Area; and from the National Tramway Museum by courtesy of the Tramway Museum Society (through Chris Gent).

Particular thanks go to London Guildhall Library, and to Cambridge University, especially Neville Taylor of the Photographic and Illustration Service for processing illustrations, and the University Library (Periodicals Department and Map Room).

Readers who would like to receive occasional updates and corrections are invited to contact *geoffrey.skelsey@btinternet.com*

8.2 Bibliography

The authoritative books by W.J.K. Davies are the finest sources of detailed information concerning the Vicinal and are particularly acknowledged.

Karl Baedeker *Handbook for Travellers, Belgium and Holland* (1910);
–: *–Belgium and Holland*, revised and augmented edition (1919);
–: *–Belgium and Luxemburg* [sic] (1931).

Jos Block *Rollend Materieel bij de Burtspoorwegen 1885-1991* (Brussel 1997).

Rose E.B. Coombs *Before Endeavours Fade* (London 1983) [survey of the Western Front 1914 – 18].

W.J.K. Davies *100 Years of the Belgian Vicinal 1885-1985* (Broxbourne 1984) [includes rolling stock details];
–: *The Vicinal Story 1885-1991* (Scarborough 2006);
–: *Light Railways* (London 1964);
–: *Light Railways of the First World War* (Newton Abbot 1967);
–: *Minor Railways of France* (East Harling, Norfolk 2000).

R. Dieudonné *Lignes de la Cote* (Bruxelles 1987) [good general history].

A. Dijkers and H.G. Hesselink *De stoomtrams op de Zuid-Hollandse eilanden en in Zeeland* (Rotterdam 1973) [SBM Tramway].

M.R.D. Foot *SOE in the Low Countries* (London 2001).

Herman van't Hoogerhuijs *Trammaterieel in Nederland en België* (Alkmaar 1996).

Luc Koenot et al *Flash 1996 Belgique* (Third edition, Bruxelles 1995);
- –: Flash 2006 *Atlas des Tramways, Metros, et Trolleybus Belges* (Fourth edition, Bruxelles 2006) [comprehensive modern details and track plan].

Frits van der Gragt et al *Couleurs Vicinales* (Breil-sur-Roya 2008) [includes tabulated fleet list].

Roland Marganne et al *Le Métro Léger de Charleroi* (Liège 2000) [BN-type history].

Carlos Van den Ostende and Willy Patten *50 ans de PCC belges*, Part I (Lentzweiler n.d. [c. 1999] [pp. 25 – 36, trials of PCC No 10419].

Société Royale Belge de Géographie *Itinéraire de la Cote et de son Arrière Pays* (Series Hommes et Paysages 10, (Bruxelles n.d. [c. 1996]).

Transport Tourism Ontspanning (TTO): Dirk Eveleens Maarse et al (eds) *Elektrische Trams aan de Belgische Kust* ([Brugge] 1996) [exhaustive rolling stock history].

R[aymond] Vancraeynest *De Tram Maakte de Kust, 1885 - 1985* (Oostende n.d. [c.1985]) [a superb detailed history].

Periodicals

Chemins de Fer Regionaux et Urbains (especially No 197, 1986)
L'Étincelle
La Voix du Nord
Modern Tramway
Nos Vicinaux
Tram 2000
Tramways and Urban Transit

Maps

The track plans by the late J.C. Gillham of tramways in and around Knokke (1949) and Oostende (1957) are valuable, and he kindly supplied copies before his death in March 2009. Of great historical interest are the military maps of western Belgium published in Great Britain by the War Office to 1:100,000 scale (1911); and in Germany by Marsa-Karten-Verlag to 1:200,000 scale (c.1915): both show Vicinal lines. A detailed plan of Belgian railways (including outline of the NMVB/SNCV) has been published by *Le Groupement Belge pour la Promotion et l'Exploitation Touristique du Transport Ferroviare asbl* (Liège [c.1979]). Successive editions of Michelin's 1:200,000 map of the coastal area are useful. Baedeker's guides contained accurate large scale plans of Oostende and Blankenberge as well as a regularly-revised general map of the Coast to 1:200,000 scale (including, surprisingly, an updated version published in the English 1919 re-issue).

Websites and visiting the Coast

Some information about the tramway is available on the world wide web, although there is unfortunately as yet no full historical site.

The De Lijn official site *(http://www.dekusttram.be/)* contains important information for visitors, including current timetables and ticket details in Flemish. Details of train services to and from the coastal towns are obtainable in English from the admirable Belgian National Railways (NMBS) at *http://www.b-rail.be/main/E* . Useful and economical weekend tickets are available permitting travel outwards to one coastal terminus, returning from another. Visitors from Great Britain should note that Eurostar (NMBS is an operating partner) include travel to and from any Belgian station in their London – Brussels fares, such journeys to be completed within twenty-four hours. Economical hotels in Brugge as well as Oostende are bookable on line (e.g. on *www.hrs.de*) or through travel agents. Motorists can easily reach the Coast via ferries to Dunkerque, detailed on *www.day-tripper.net*, but it is unfortunately no longer possible for passengers without cars to travel from southern England direct to Belgium by sea.

There is some published information in Flemish on long-term light rail projects, including the following sites:

Light rail prospects

(published by the government office 'Afdeling Beleid Mobiliteit en Verkeersveiligheid', [Mobility and Road Safety Policy Department] April 2008)
http://www.mobielvlaanderen.be/studies/lightrail
(accessed 19 May 2009)

Long-term plans for regional transport

http://nl.wikipedia.org/wiki/Neptunusplan
(15 May 2009)

The following unofficial sites are also worth visiting:

'Belgian Coastal Tram' in *Wikipedia* at http://en.wikipedia.org/wiki/Belgian_coast_tram
(12 May 2009)

'Kustram' at http://www.kusttram.eu/
(14 May 2009)

About the Authors

The authors have collaborated previously on contributions to *Tramways and Urban Transit, Tramway Review,* and *l'Etincelle,* and recently on the LRTA's extended work on the Brussels Tramways since 1945 *A Tramway Reborn* (2008).

Geoffrey Skelsey took his first Belgian tram ride in 1959 (along the coast) and has not stopped visiting the country since. After graduating in English from St Catharine's College, Cambridge and subsequently studying law, he spent his career in the public service and was appointed by HM The Queen to the Royal Victorian Order and by HM The King of Spain to the *Orden del Merito Civil*. He writes regularly for several periodicals and works as a political researcher. He has previously published *The NET Success Story: Nottingham's New Trams* with the LRTA.

Yves-Laurent Hansart was born and educated in Brussels and runs his own computer business in the city. He is actively involved in the *Association Pour La Sauvegarde du Vicinal* (ASVi) and its superb operating museum at Thuin, near Charleroi.

Light Rail Transit Association
Advocating modern tramways and urban light rail transit

The Light Rail Transit Association is an international organisation dedicated to campaigning for better fixed-track public transport, in particular tramways (usually on-street) and light rail (usually off-street but very accessible).

Membership of the LRTA is open equally to professional organisations, transport planners and individuals with a particular interest in the subject. Members receive free of charge by post *Tramways & Urban Transit*, the all-colour monthly A4-size magazine, as part of their subscription. With tramway and light rail systems being adopted not only in Europe but world-wide, this high-quality journal features topical articles and extensive news coverage, also trade news, book reviews and readers' letters. Details of local meetings in the British Isles are included. Supplementing the above, *Tramway Review* (quarterly) is mainly devoted to historical material.

LRTA Officers (many with transport industry experience) form part of an extensive network of light rail and tramway information sources. The LRTA library is also available, details on request.

For further copies of this book:
www.lrta.info/shop
(LRTA c/o Eaglethorpe Barns, Warmington, Peterborough PE8 6TJ)

LRTA Subscriptions & Membership information:
membership@lrta.org
(38 Wolseley Road, Sale, Greater Manchester M33 7AU)

General LRTA Enquiries:
secretary@lrta.org
(138 Radnor Avenue, Welling DA16 2BY)

General LRTA Publications enquiries:
publications@lrta.org
(14 Prae Close, St. Albans AL3 4SF)

FOR FURTHER INFORMATION VISIT THE LRTA WEBSITE: *www.lrta.org*